ROSE
DISCIPLESHIP SER

GOING

SPIRITUAL PRACTICES

R SE
PUBLISHING

Going: Spiritual Practices
Rose Discipleship Series
©2021 Rose Publishing

Published by Rose Publishing
An imprint of Tyndale House Ministries
Carol Stream, Illinois
www.hendricksonrose.com

ISBN 978-164938-019-7

Contributing Editor: Len Woods
Cover design by Sergio Urquiza

Images used under license from Shutterstock.com: Collin Quinn Lomax, page 5; Jaromir Chalabala, 25; Monkey Business Images, 44, 72; KucherAv, 55; P Maxwell Photography, 62; Jantanee Runpranomkorn, 90; grafvision, 92

Printed in the United States of America
May 2021, 1st printing

Contents

Topic 1
A Disciple Serves: Reaching Out and Serving Like Jesus 5

Topic 2
Worship: Bringing God Glory in All You Do 15

Topic 3
Solitude & Silence: Learning to Quiet Your Soul..25

Topic 4
Bible Reading & Study: Being Rooted in God's Truth................................32

Topic 5
Prayer: Communing with God 44

Topic 6
Fasting: Cultivating an Appetite for the Things of God................................54

Topic 7
Giving: Understanding Generosity and Stewardship...................................61

Topic 8
Spiritual Gifts: Laying Down Your Life for Others.......................................71

Topic 9
Evangelism: Sharing the Message of Your New Life in Christ 80

Topic 10
Missions: Embracing God's Heart for the World 91

Leader Guide.. 100

What Is Discipleship?

A disciple is a person who follows Jesus—to *know* Jesus and his teachings, to *grow* more like Jesus, and to *go* for Jesus, serving others and making new disciples. Simply put, the goal of discipleship is to become more like Jesus.

Healthy discipleship is always integrated. What we *know* in our heads should permeate our hearts and help us grow. *Growing* in the faith can't be separated from knowing truth and going forth to serve others and honor God. *Going* is tied together with knowing God's truth and growing to have the right heart attitude.

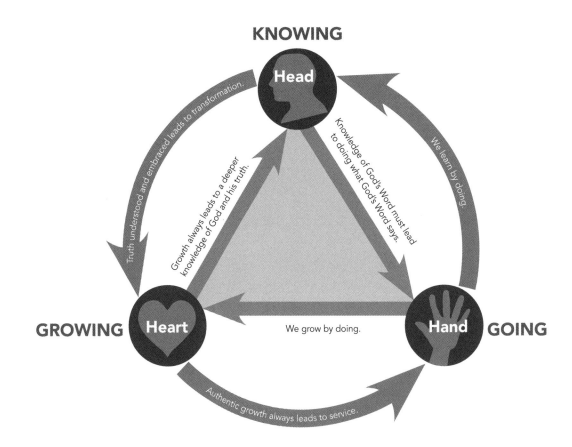

The ten topics in this book focus on *going* forth in service, evangelism, and spiritual practices. Other books in this series focus on *knowing* the essential truths about God, the Bible, the gospel, and the church, and *growing* in the fruits of the Spirit and other traits that help us become more like Christ.

Topic 1: A Disciple Serves

Reaching Out and Serving Like Jesus

"For even the Son of Man did not come to
be served, but to serve, and to give his life
as a ransom for many."

—Mark 10:45

For many believers, faith is like a precious family heirloom. It's ours, and we're thrilled to have it! We know it's extremely valuable. We even mention it from time to time in conversations. But we don't always use it in daily life. Like grandma's china that remains out-of-sight in a large box in the garage, modern faith for many believers can be real, but not exactly relevant.

Contrast that idea of faith with the kind of faith portrayed in the Bible. In the Scriptures, faith isn't something you merely *have*; it's something you *live*. You don't stop with pondering it—you practice it! Biblical faith is less of a noun and more of a verb. The kind of believing Jesus advocated is active and obvious to others.

In other words, we shouldn't expect following Jesus to make for an easy life. Gospel faith is restless and active. It comforts us, but doesn't ever let us get too comfortable. Jesus made it clear there's work to be done. We have a mission to accomplish. Among Christ's final words to his disciples: "Go and make disciples of all nations" (Matthew 28:18–20).

Bible Study

1. Take a few moments to read and carefully consider these Bible passages that call us to action, compel us to go, and challenge us to embrace the same servant lifestyle and disciple-making mission that Jesus embraced:

   ▶ "In the same way, let your good deeds shine out for all to see, so that everyone will praise your heavenly Father" (Jesus, in Matthew 5:16, NLT).

   ▶ "He [Jesus] told them, 'The harvest is plentiful, but the workers are few. Ask the Lord of the harvest, therefore, to send out workers into his harvest field. Go! I am sending you out like lambs among wolves" (Jesus, in Luke 10:2–3).

   ▶ "But you will receive power when the Holy Spirit comes upon you. And you will be my witnesses, telling people about me everywhere—in Jerusalem, throughout Judea, in Samaria, and to the ends of the earth" (Jesus, in Acts 1:8, NLT).

   ▶ "Each of you should use whatever gift you have received to serve others, as faithful stewards of God's grace in its various forms" (1 Peter 4:10).

   What are your thoughts when you read such commands to do good deeds? To go and be a worker in the Lord's harvest field? To be a witness? To serve others?

   ----

2. According to the New Testament, discipleship is the lifelong process of following Jesus in order to become like him. If this is so, we can't just pursue the *character* of Jesus, we also have to take up the *mission* of Jesus and serve others. After all, 1 John 2:6 says, "Whoever claims to live in him must live as Jesus did."

   Read:

   ▶ Matthew 10:40

   ▶ Mark 12:6

   ▶ Luke 4:18

How does Jesus describe himself in each of these passages? What does this mean for followers of Jesus?

---

3. The apostle Paul writes, "train yourself to be godly" (1 Timothy 4:7; the NASB renders this phrase "discipline yourself for the purpose of godliness"). What do you think Paul means? Why do you think this is hard?

It's worth noting that the present tense verb Paul uses here (translated "train" or "discipline") is the Greek word from which we get our English term "gymnasium." In other words, Paul is insisting that we give our souls a regular workout! Just as we go to the gym to exercise our bodies, we are to engage in spiritual exercises that will strengthen and firm up our souls.

Such spiritual practices (or holy habits) are often called spiritual disciplines. They are everything from solitude and silence, Bible reading and prayer, to giving and service. *Any regular activity that we intentionally practice in order to open ourselves up to the Lord's transforming presence can be considered a spiritual discipline.*

Just as physical exercise leads to strength and health and fitness, in the same way spiritual exercises, properly understood and utilized, can help us grow to become like Christ.

A wrong view of spiritual disciplines	A right view of spiritual disciplines
Something for monks, nuns, and church leaders	Something for every Christ-follower
Something I am supposed to do for God	A way I can be with God
The goal is doing	The goal is becoming
Performed out of guilt (a "have to")	Practiced out of gladness (a "get to")
An end in themselves	A means to an end—being in God's transforming presence
A sign of spiritual maturity	A means to spiritual maturity

4. **Single-minded. Focused. Committed. Intentional.** We could describe Christ's life in all of these ways. So how, practically speaking, can a follower of Jesus today (with a job, bills, school, friends, family, etc.) embrace these same priorities in life?

_____

_____

_____

_____

_____

A healthy approach to discipleship includes both being and doing. It calls for "with-ness" (i.e., being with Jesus) and witness (going for Jesus). Following Jesus is both personal and interpersonal. It encompasses both beliefs and behavior. It results in both internal transformation and external impact. We receive from God and from others, then we share what we have received.

The diagram on the following page illustrates this truth.

"BECOMING A DISCIPLE" is

trusting in Christ alone for salvation and following Jesus in order to *know* Jesus and his teachings; to *grow* more like Jesus; and to *go* for Jesus, serving others and making new disciples. We do this by continually opening up ourselves to God's transforming presence and by getting regular input from other disciples.

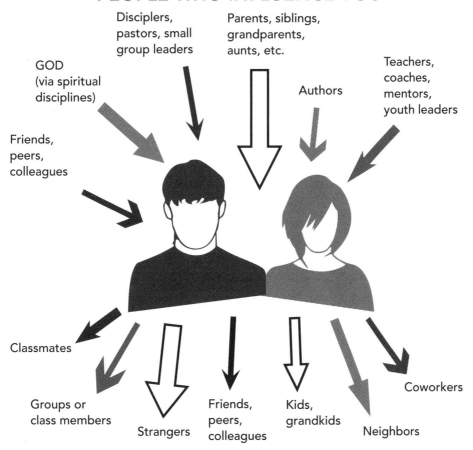

PEOPLE WHO INFLUENCE YOU

Disciplers, pastors, small group leaders

Parents, siblings, grandparents, aunts, etc.

GOD (via spiritual disciplines)

Authors

Teachers, coaches, mentors, youth leaders

Friends, peers, colleagues

Classmates

Groups or class members

Strangers

Friends, peers, colleagues

Kids, grandkids

Neighbors

Coworkers

PEOPLE WHOM YOU INFLUENCE

"MAKING DISCIPLES" is

leading others to trust in Christ alone for salvation and to orient their lives around the three-fold desire to *know* Jesus and his teaching; to *grow* more like Jesus; and to *go* for Jesus, serving others and making new disciples. We do this by serving, and giving our lives away, as Jesus did. We share with and invest in others the wisdom, truth, experiences, insights, resources, skills, abilities, etc. God has given to us.

Personally embracing Christ's mission to go and make disciples may involve the following:

➤ **Rejecting** the self-centeredness of our culture and embracing the self-less, servant mindset modeled by Jesus (Philippians 2)

➤ **Understanding** you have been saved for a life of good works that match the unique ways God has created or "wired" you (see Ephesians 2:8–10)

➤ **Letting** your light shine out among neighbors, coworkers, friends, etc., by doing those good works in the power of God's Spirit (Matthew 5:16)

➤ **Discovering**, **understanding**, and **utilizing** your God-given abilities to serve and build up the Body of Christ (Romans 12; 1 Corinthians 12; Ephesians 4; 1 Peter 4)

➤ **Getting** equipped to minister to others (Ephesians 4:11–13)

➤ **Taking** the truth, training, and blessings God has given you and turning around and investing that in others (2 Timothy 2:2)

➤ **Learning** how to give a reason "for the hope that is in you," then sharing your own story of how the Good News of Jesus has changed your life (1 Peter 3:15, NASB)

Servanthood Action Scale

Examine each pair of actions or attitudes in the scale below. Where do you see yourself?

Doing occasional acts of service	⇄	Having a servant's heart
Serving in "official" capacities	⇄	Serving in "unofficial" capacities
Helping when asked	⇄	Noticing needs and taking the initiative to help
Focusing on needed tasks	⇄	Focusing on people in need
Serving according to what others need	⇄	Serving according to my gifts and passions
The gift of serving (some believers)	⇄	The command to serve (all believers)
"Out front" visible service	⇄	"Behind-the-scenes" invisible service
Serving within the church	⇄	Serving outside the church

5. Looking at the pairs of actions and attitudes in the scale on page 61, write down where you are now and where you would like to be. What action steps will you take to get where you want to be?

_____

_____

_____

_____

_____

_____

6. Consider your experiences in serving Christ: engaging in ministry, going on mission trips, etc. Describe an experience you felt good about and one you did not feel was successful. What did you learn from these experiences?

_____

_____

_____

_____

_____

_____

_____

_____

_____

_____

_____

_____

_____

_____

Take-Home Reflections

In the gospel of John, Jesus described himself as "sent" by God in multiple passages. These are listed below. Look up the verses, read and underline them so you can easily remind yourself who sent Jesus.

Clearly Jesus saw himself as being on a mission from God!

❏ John 3:34   ❏ John 8:29

❏ John 4:34   ❏ John 8:42

❏ John 5:23–24   ❏ John 9:4

❏ John 5:30   ❏ John 10:36

❏ John 5:37–38   ❏ John 12:44–45

❏ John 6:29   ❏ John 12:49

❏ John 6:38–39   ❏ John 14:24

❏ John 6:44   ❏ John 15:21

❏ John 6:57   ❏ John 16:5

❏ John 7:16   ❏ John 17:3

❏ John 7:18   ❏ John 17:8

❏ John 7:28–29   ❏ John 17:18

❏ John 7:33   ❏ John 17:21

❏ John 8:16   ❏ John 17:23

❏ John 8:18   ❏ John 17:25

❏ John 8:26   ❏ John 20:21

▶ His single, declared objective was to accomplish the will of his Father in heaven (John 4:34; 5:30; 6:38–39)

▶ He came, he said, not to be served, but to serve and give his life away as a sacrifice (Mark 10:45). His stated purpose was "to seek and save those who are lost" (Luke 19:10, NLT).

▶ To what end? To accomplish his announced intention to "build my church" (Matthew 16:18).

Life Application

An important part of discipleship is learning how to apply God's truths to your life. Below are just a few ways you can start thinking about what you've learned and apply it to your daily life.

1. Memorize our memory verse, Mark 10:45.

2. Work through the personal "Your Inventory of Abilities that Meet Needs" list on page 13. What are some of the unique ways God has gifted you and/or placed desires within you to make an eternal difference? How might your answers serve as clues to the role you can play in serving Christ and making disciples?

3. Wrestle with one or two of these questions:

   ▶ What from the "Your Inventory of Abilities that Meet Needs" list surprises you? What avenue of serving God or making disciples would you like to explore more fully?

   ▶ Who are the people who have poured into your life—and helped you grow spiritually? How exactly did they do that?

   ▶ Do you have people into whom you are intentionally investing? Who? What does that look like?

   ▶ What would you say to someone who said, "I really want to grow in my faith, but I'm honestly not that interested in 'serving others,'" or "I'm not qualified to 'minister' to someone else"?

   ▶ The New Testament teaches that God gives *each* and *every* believer in Christ *spiritual abilities* for accomplishing His work in the world (Romans 12; 1 Corinthians 12; Ephesians 4; 1 Peter 4). Experience further reveals that we all have *natural talents* and *unique passions* for making a difference. Do you agree that God will get the most glory, and we will feel most fulfilled if we minister, serve, and make disciples in ways that use our strengths and involve our interests? Why or why not?

Your Inventory of Abilities that Meet Needs

I believe God has *gifted* me to *(check all that apply)* . . .

❑ **Invite/recruit:** Reaching out to others to encourage their participation in relationships, groups, or events where they can grow spiritually and serve others

❑ **Meet/greet/host people:** Taking the initiative to show hospitality and make people feel welcomed and accepted

❑ **Pray for others:** The consistent holy habit of interceding for others

❑ **Organize/administrate/plan:** Bringing order to chaos, and handling details to accomplish a task or pull off an event

❑ **Show compassion:** Noticing hurting people and moving into their lives to tangibly demonstrate the love of Christ

❑ **Listen/counsel:** Taking time to hear the hearts and hurts of others and help them process what God is saying to them

❑ **Mentor others:** Coming alongside others so as to share knowledge, model life skills, and/or impart wisdom gleaned from ones' own successes and failures

❑ **Be crafty:** The ability to sew, build, decorate, etc. to produce beautiful and useful objects for events that bless others

❑ **Shepherd others:** A knack for coming alongside those who are encountering difficulties in life to comfort and guide

❑ **Train others in specific skills:** The ability to pass on the info and skills needed for success in a specific area of life

❑ **Find and distribute important facts:** Making sure people have the information they need to make progress in the faith

❑ **Inspire others through artistic endeavors:** The ability to sing, play an instrument, paint, sculpt, write, act, dance, make videos, or take pictures and in that, to communicate God's truth creatively, beautifully and memorably

❑ **Encourage and motivate:** The rare ability to impart new hope and courage to those who have become discouraged

❑ **Share my faith:** The ability to effectively show and tell the good news of Christ's offer to forgive sin and give eternal life

❑ **Help with simple tasks:** The willingness to lend a hand with various projects or random needs that do not require special skills or expertise

❑ **Show mercy:** Demonstrating love, acceptance, and kindness to those who are filled with shame

❑ **Share or give:** Cheerfully donating one's time, energy, effort, resources and/or funds to worthwhile kingdom efforts

❑ **Lead teams/groups/projects:** Guiding people to the successful and satisfying completion of a specific task

❑ **Provide technical and mechanical assistance:** The ability to keep gadgets and gizmos from breaking and/or to fix them when they do stop working

❑ **Lead discussions/teach:** Serving as a catalyst for helping others understand and apply biblical truth

❑ **Cook or bake:** Serving Christ by serving enjoyable meals

Bringing God Glory in All You Do

"So whether you eat or drink or whatever
you do, do it all for the glory of God."
—1 Corinthians 10:31

Ask a few people what the word "worship" means to them, and you're likely to get a wide variety of answers. And each of these can be an important *part* of a person's worship of God.

What Does Worship Mean?

Common Responses	What That Means
"It's what we call the gathering at our church on Sunday mornings."	Worship is a meeting on a certain day at a certain place at a certain time.
"It's what we do at church between the welcome and announcements and the sermon."	Worship is spiritual music—it's singing songs with other Christians.
"Worship is spiritual music—it's singing songs with other Christians."	Worship is a certain body posture or an outward act of enthusiasm.
"It's turning away from secular stuff and focusing on spiritual truth."	Worship is a retreat from earthly realities.

"Every man is bound somewhere, somehow, to a throne, to a government, to an authority, to something that is supreme, to something to which he offers sacrifice, and burns incense, and bends the knee."
—G. Campbell Morgan

As has been stated before, a disciple is a person who follows Jesus—to *know* Jesus and his teaching; to *grow* more like Jesus; and to *go* for Jesus, serving others and making new disciples.

In other words, discipleship involves learning new insights, taking on a new character, and engaging in new behaviors. Some of these new behaviors are referred to as spiritual disciplines or practices.

When we think of the practices that shape a disciple, it's good to start with *worship*.

1. What words, images, etc. come to mind when you think of the word "worship"?

_____

_____

_____

First, we'll look at the meaning of that word.

Worship Defined and Described

Read these verses, one from the Old Testament, and one from the New Testament:

▶ "Come, let us worship and bow down, let us kneel before the LORD our Maker." (Psalm 95:6, NASB)

▶ "But the hour is coming, and is now here, when the true worshipers will worship the Father in spirit and truth, for the Father is seeking such people to worship him. God is spirit, and those who worship him must worship in spirit and truth." (John 4:23–24, ESV)

The Hebrew word translated *worship* in Psalm 95:6 is *shachah*. It means literally "to bow down." The idea is bending low or prostrating oneself as a way of giving honor or paying homage or expressing devotion.

The Greek word translated worship in John 4 is *proskyne*. It also conveys this same idea of bowing with respect and devotion (see Matthew 2:11, 4:9, and 28:9).

What about our English word "worship"? It is derived from the Old English term "worthship"—literally, having worth or value.

> "It is not a thing which a man can decide, whether he will be a worshiper or not, a worshiper he must be, the only question is what will he worship? Every man worships—is a born worshiper."
> —Frederick Robertson

Put all those meanings together and in the most basic sense:

Worship is assigning worth and value to someone (or something), and then—out of respect, gratitude, affection, devotion, or fear— bowing one's life before that someone (or something).

Bible Study

Based on our definition and description of worship, there are two important implications:

1. Everyone worships someone or something.

2. A disciple seeks to worship God and God alone.

Everyone Worships Someone or Something.

If worship is about ascribing value, then every person does that. Everybody has things—people or goals or dreams—he or she considers valuable—and usually one "something" viewed as having supreme worth. So it's never a question of "*Will* we worship?" but rather, "*Who* or *what* will we worship?"

Think of all the "created" things to which people can and do assign worth or ascribe value:

▶ Family

▶ Marriage

▶ Educational credentials

▶ Children

▶ Grandchildren

▶ A boyfriend or girlfriend

▶ Friendships

▶ A job, career, work

▶ A financial portfolio

▶ A dream (retirement, having your own business, vacation home, etc.)

▶ A political ideology

▶ The success of a sports team

▶ Health

▶ Fitness

▶ Physical appearance

▶ Acclaim

▶ The approval of others

▶ Sexual gratification

▶ Accomplishments

▶ Winning (being the best at everything)

▶ Popularity

▶ A reputation or image

> "He who has not learned to worship will find God and this world wearisome. If you've trusted in Christ as your Savior, but you've really not learned to worship God, chances are you have found the Christian life disappointing."
> —Ravi Zacharias

Many of these items are good things—even blessings from God! But they are not as important as God. We must never let *good* things become *ultimate* things in our hearts.

Why Does God Command Us to Worship Him?

Isn't that vain and egotistical?

The eternal Triune God doesn't need our worship. He is complete. He lacks nothing. He is neither threatened nor diminished if humans refuse or fail to worship him.

God does command worship, however, because it is:

- Fitting
- Fulfilling

Worship of God is fitting.

As the perfect and majestic one, God deserves worship. He is worthy of all praise. Imagine how shocked you would be to watch someone spurn an exquisite gourmet feast prepared by the world's best chef, only to turn around and rave over a mediocre fast-food meal. To fail to worship the one who is worthy of infinite praise is an infinite scandal! This is why the heavens themselves shout the glory of God (Psalm 19:1). This is why God's throne is surrounded by angelic beings who forever worship him (Revelation 4:8).

God saying, "Worship me" isn't vain; it's right. It's common sense.

Worship of God is fulfilling.

The other reason God commands us to worship him is for our benefit. When we praise God we find satisfaction and joy. C. S. Lewis talked about this—how expressing our awe or wonder or appreciation to God "completes the enjoyment." Imagine not being able to cheer your favorite team after a last-second victory, or not being allowed to express affection to your beloved. Our delight and joy would be diminished.

2. In what ways is this idea that everyone worships someone or something a new concept to you?

A Disciple Worships God and God Alone

3. Look at these two verses, one from the Old Testament and one from the New:

▶ "Bring all who claim me as their God, for I have made them for my glory. It was I who created them.'" (Isaiah 43:7, NLT)

▶ "For in him all things were created." (Colossians 1:16)

According to these passages, why did God create us?

_____

_____

_____

_____

4. What does it mean to live for the glory of God?

_____

_____

_____

_____

What Psalms Teaches Us About Worship

"For me, the key to worship is simply quiet, undistracted time with my eyes closed. By setting aside a certain time of my day for God—and God alone—I am indicating in the best way I know that he is important to me. I will sit and love him whether I feel his presence or not. Of course, the Bible assures me he is with me, always, whether I sense his presence or not."
—43-year-old woman

The Old Testament Book of Psalms was the "hymn book" for the Jewish people, including Jesus. These 150 prayer-songs are beloved because they speak to every situation and emotion of life. They show that God is worthy of our worship—our attention, allegiance, affection, and adoration—no matter what we're facing.

When you read the psalms you'll notice they include loud, expressive worship and quiet introspective meditation. Whether songs of protest or praise, an individual reeling in terror or a nation rejoicing in triumph, in the psalms we see God's people:

- ▶ Bowing down before God (Psalm 95:6)

- ▶ Seeking his face (Psalm 105:3–4)

- ▶ Waiting for the Lord (Psalm 33:20–21)

- ▶ Dwelling in his house (Psalm 27:4)

- ▶ Lifting hands (Psalm 134:2)

- ▶ Shouting to him (Psalm 47:1)

- ▶ Singing to him (Psalm 104:33)

In short, the psalms show us that worship is not simply attending a "worship service" at some kind of "worship facility" and singing "worship songs." Worship isn't an event so much as it's a mindset, a posture of life. It's choosing to make God central. It's cultivating the moment-by-moment practice of looking to God and saying from the heart, "I want to live for your glory!"

- ▶ In wondrous moments it's exclaiming, "Wow! You are amazing!"

- ▶ In tough situations it's crying out, "I need you!"

- ▶ In good times it's saying, "Thank you!"

- ▶ In faith-testing circumstances it's whispering, "Okay (gulp!) I am trusting you."

Okay, now comes the fun part.

How Do We Engage in this Practice of Worship?

In the same way we have different personalities and relational styles, different strengths and interests, so we have different ways of worshiping or connecting with God.

In his book, *Sacred Pathways,* author Gary Thomas shows how, for some two thousand years, Christians have expressed their enjoyment and worship of God through a variety of "pathways."

Though there are surely others, he cites nine primary ways people draw near to God and express their love and devotion to him:

> "A friend of mine who was in medical school took me into the 'cadaver room' where she and other first year students learned about human anatomy by exploring bodies that had been donated to science. When she opened a 'body bag' to reveal a dissected human form, I almost dropped to my knees. I was struck, not by nausea but by awe. The complexity and intricacy of our bodies—we really are, as the Bible says, 'fearfully and wonderfully made.' In that moment, I worshiped, maybe more than I ever have in a church."—30-year-old man

- ▶ *Naturalists* are those who feel inspired to love God when they are out-of-doors, in natural settings.

- *Sensates* worship with their senses. They appreciate beautiful worship services that involve their sight (art), smell (incense), and ears (music).

- *Ascetics* prefer to worship in quiet solitude and simplicity.

- *Activists* adore God through confronting evil and battling injustice in the world.

- *Caregivers* worship by loving others and meeting their needs.

- *Traditionalists* draw closer to God and worship him through rituals, liturgy, symbols, and unchanging structures.

- *Enthusiasts* worship through expressive celebration.

- *Contemplatives* love God through peaceful adoration.

- *Intellectuals* praise God by studying with their minds.

5. What would you say is your primary "pathway" of worship?

_____

_____

_____

6. What would be the value of sometimes participating in worship pathways that are not your first preference?

_____

_____

_____

_____

7. What worship advice would you give a person who says, "I don't sense God. In fact, I doubt his presence in my life right now"?

_____

_____

_____

_____

Outside-the-Box Worship

Anything is worship when it is done with an eye on God and with gratitude to God.

Try these different ways of worship:

▶ Take a walk or hike and soak up God's creation.

▶ Sit and gawk at a sunset.

▶ Sing. Being off-key or pitchy is irrelevant, which is why Psalm 95 tells us, "Make a joyful noise!" (Psalm 95:1, ESV) and not "Perform a beautiful song."

▶ Climb a tree.

▶ Write a blog post that would make God smile.

▶ Marvel at the complexity of science or the precision of an algebraic formula.

▶ Study a leaf, a flower, a caterpillar, a rock.

▶ Laughing with your toddler as he or she splashes in a puddle.

▶ Lie in a meadow on a cloudless night and watch shooting stars.

▶ Make or create something: a short story, a poem, a drawing, a painting, a sculpture, a video, a great meal, a woodworking project, an article of clothing, etc.

8. What are some other new and different ways you can think of to turn your heart to God and show your love and gratitude for him?

_____

_____

_____

_____

9. How do you feel God's Spirit prompting you to alter your worship views or practices as a result of this study?

_____

_____

_____

_____

Take-Home Reflections

Quick Reminders About Worship

Thoughts or Feelings	Way You Can React
When feeling blah or sad	Don't pretend to be upbeat when you're not. Worship isn't a pep rally. It's being your authentic self in the presence of God. As the psalms show us, sometimes that means crying out in despair (not laughing, smiling, and jumping around).
When wondering if you're doing it "right"	First, there's no single "right" way to worship. Second, God is gracious and knows your heart. When you make a genuine effort to worship God you are worshipping God. Desiring to love God is loving God.
When you can't sense God's presence	Pray something like this: "God, you promise in your Word that you are always with me. That doesn't feel true right now, but I choose to trust what you say, rather than what I sense. Thank you for being right here."
When you feel dry or stuck	It's okay to have bad days: Don't be hard on yourself. Every worshiper experiences this. People go up and down depending on the amount of sleep or good food or how healthy they are or how much stress they are under.
When you don't feel like singing—maybe due to being tone deaf or having hearing problems or over-sensitive ears	Focus on the lyrics, or be encouraged in your heart by watching others love God through song.

Life Application

An important part of discipleship is learning how to apply God's truths to your life. Below are just a few ways you can start thinking about what you've learned and apply it to your daily life.

1. Memorize our memory verse, 1 Corinthians 10:31.

   "So whether you eat or drink or whatever you do, do it all for the glory of God."

2. Ponder the chart "Worship Myths and Truths" on the next page.

3. Wrestle with one or two of these questions:

   ▶ In what new way could you worship God this week?

▶ Repetition can get stale, so how can you mix up your worship time?

   ✦ A different Bible verse?

   ✦ Reading a book about God?

   ✦ Singing?

   ✦ Focusing on one attribute of God?

▶ What three things are you grateful for today?

▶ Where are you most dependent on God?

▶ Describe a time you felt God's power or closeness.

▶ Finish this sentence: I find myself worshipping and praising God when . . .

Worship Myths and Truths

Worship Myth	Worship Truth
Worship is a gathering at a certain time and in a certain place.	Worship is an all-day, every-day mindset. It's bowing down to God and his purpose for our lives.
That we "go" to worship.	We "live" worship, and bring it with us—or not.
Worship is a handful of "spiritual" activities such as singing, praying, taking communion, hearing sermons, etc.	All of life—even secular activities—can be worship, if we do them for the glory of God. For example, enjoying the beautiful world God created by taking a hike.
Worship is about externals such as music, song choices, body posture, how good the band or worship leader is, how expressive the congregation is, etc.	Worship is about the heart. It is setting aside quiet time alone and saying, "God, I love you. God, I trust you. God, I praise you."
God-honoring worship means having or coming away with a certain feeling.	God-honoring worship is approaching God by faith, and "in the spirit and in truth" (John 4:24) whether having any sensations or not.
I am the judge of whether a time of worship was worthwhile.	I am to participate in worship—and leave judgments about its quality to God. Attempting to worship God *is* to worship God. God accepts our attempts, no matter how feeble.
One kind of worship is better than others.	An infinite God can be worshiped in a variety of ways (privately, publicly; individually, corporately; silently, loudly; etc.)—whatever works for your personality and situation. No one way of worshiping is better than any other.

Topic 3: Solitude & Silence

Learning to Quiet Your Soul

"This is what the Sovereign LORD,
the Holy One of Israel, says:
'In repentance and rest is your salvation,
in quietness and trust is your strength.'"
—Isaiah 30:15

Two things are true:

▶ We are the most *connected* generation ever.

▶ Ours is the *loudest* culture in human history.

Think about it . . . we have smart phones that can do about everything but serve us a

cappuccino! With wireless technology, we can stream music and movies (and pretty much anything else) from the Internet—twenty-four hours a day, seven days a week—from just about anywhere on the planet. Would you like to sit in a bustling coffee shop and listen to your favorite band while you FaceTime with a friend on the opposite coast, text back and forth with your mom, *and* keep an eye on your Twitter feed? No problem.

But at what cost? What's all this doing to our souls? Are we addicted to noise? And is our constant connection to culture hurting our connection with God?

Here's a third true thing: As we follow Jesus to know him and his teachings and as we grow to become more like him in character, we must also do the things Jesus did. We must engage in holy habits, or spiritual disciplines. These are integral to God's mission of transformation—our own lives and the lives of others. Two of these holy habits are *solitude* and *silence*.

Bible Study

What the Bible Tells Us About Solitude

For Jesus, time in solitude was a top priority. Consider these passages, one from each of the four gospels:

- ▶ "After he had dismissed them, he went up on a mountainside by himself to pray. Later that night, he was there alone" (Matthew 14:23).

- ▶ "Very early in the morning, while it was still dark, Jesus got up, left the house and went off to a solitary place, where he prayed" (Mark 1:35).

- ▶ "Once when Jesus was praying in private and his disciples were with him, he asked them, 'Who do the crowds say I am?'" (Luke 9:18).

- ▶ "Jesus, knowing that they intended to come and make him king by force, withdrew again to a mountain by himself" (John 6:15).

> "We are so afraid of silence that we chase ourselves from one event to the next in order not to have to spend a moment alone with ourselves, in order not to have to look at ourselves in the mirror."
> —Dietrich Bonhoeffer

1. What conclusions do you draw from those verses?

_____

_____

_____

_____

_____

Solitude is a retreat—whether brief or long—from people and the distractions of modern life. It's the deliberate choice to withdraw from social interaction and daily "to do" lists so that you can enter an environment in which you can focus your undivided attention on the Father in heaven. When the Bible emphasizes solitude, it doesn't just mean "being alone." It means "being alone *with God*." This is important for at least three reasons:

Solitude Is Preparatory

Time alone with God can strengthen us for upcoming ministry or life challenges. Jesus spent almost six weeks alone in the wilderness before commencing his public ministry (Matthew 4:2).

Simple Ways to Find Solitude

Whether you need a few minutes of time alone with God or a more extended period, here are some tips:

- Set your alarm to go off thirty minutes before the others in your household wake up.
- Stay awake for thirty minutes after everyone else has gone to bed.
- If it's safe to do so, take a walk around your neighborhood after dark.
- Find a nearby park and "claim" an unused park bench.
- Utilize the guest room.
- At work, take advantage of an empty conference room during lunch.
- Park your car by a nearby lake.
- Find a study carrel in the library.
- Go sit in your deer stand, duck blind, or fishing camp.
- Borrow a friend's house who is on vacation.
- Go in your bedroom and lock the door.
- Sit and soak in the bathtub.
- Sit on the back porch in a rocking chair.
- Slip into a church or chapel during the week.

It's because of Jesus' example that many believers get up a few minutes early each day and have a devotional time, quiet time, or appointment with God. They see this as an important spiritual exercise—an opportunity to get their bearings, remember what's true, and reconnect with the lover of their souls before launching out into a crowded and loud world.

Discussion Questions

▶ What are your own devotional life habits? Do you have any?

▶ Have you ever experimented with extended times of silence or even a silent retreat? What was that like?

Solitude Is Revealing

When we are socially engaged, mixing and mingling with people, or handling all of the tasks at work or home, it's easy to become obsessed with what others think. Our minds fill with questions:

▶ *How am I coming across?*

▶ *Do they notice me?*

▶ *Do they like me?*

▶ *Do they consider me charming? Funny? Intelligent? Competent?*

▶ *Am I doing everything on my to-do list?*

▶ *Does God see me as a failure?*

Surrounded by people and jockeying for attention and acclaim, our motives and mission can morph. Instead of being our authentic selves, we become image-conscious. We are "on." We play to the crowd. We wear masks.

In solitude all that is stripped away. There's no one around to impress, no one around to fear. It's just us and the one who knows us through and through, the one who loves us fully and completely.

Solitude clarifies exactly what we've been looking to for our identities. Like Jesus in the wilderness, solitude forces us to deal with the temptation to find significance in unhealthy ways. But in addition, it helps us see that God loves us unconditionally. No matter how we've failed, he loves us and is on our side, helping us to stand up again and keep going.

Discussion Questions

▶ Is the thought of solitude *exciting* to you, *excruciating*, or something in between? Why?

▶ In recent years, researchers and writers have shed light on different personality types—For example, being an introvert versus being an extrovert. Which are you? Could that be one clue as to why you either enjoy or hate solitude?

Solitude Is Restorative

"Here then I am, far from the busy ways of men. I sit down alone; only God is here."—John Wesley

When we're tired or confused, when we have forgotten who and whose we really are, solitude can help us regain our bearings. By withdrawing, we can tune out all the other voices and hear the one voice that matters most.

In 1 Kings 19:1–4, 9–13 (NLT) we read a great example of the restorative power of solitude in the life of the prophet Elijah. After a stressful time of ministry in which he had faced down hundreds of false prophets, these events happened:

When [King] Ahab got home, he told Jezebel [his wife, the queen] everything Elijah had done, including the way he had killed all the prophets of Baal. So Jezebel sent this message to Elijah: "May the gods strike me and even kill me if by this time tomorrow I have not killed you just as you killed them."

Elijah was afraid and fled for his life. He went to Beersheba, a town in Judah, and he left his servant there. Then he went on alone into the wilderness, traveling all day. He sat down under a solitary broom tree and prayed that he might die.

But the Lord said to him, "What are you doing here, Elijah?"

Elijah replied, "I have zealously served the Lord God Almighty. But the people of Israel have broken their covenant with you, torn down your altars, and killed every one of your prophets. I am the only one left, and now they are trying to kill me, too."

"Go out and stand before me on the mountain," the Lord told him. And as Elijah stood there, the Lord passed by, and a mighty windstorm hit the mountain. It was such a terrible blast that the rocks were torn loose, but the Lord was not in the wind. After the wind there was an earthquake, but the Lord was not in the earthquake. And after the earthquake there was a fire, but the Lord was not in the fire. And after the fire there was the sound of a gentle whisper. When Elijah heard it, he wrapped his face in his cloak and went out and stood at the entrance of the cave.

And a voice said, "What are you doing here, Elijah?"

Discussion Questions

▶ The sound Elijah heard in verse 12, "a gentle whisper," is also translated as "a low whisper" (ESV), and "a gentle blowing" (NASB). What exactly do you think he heard in this solitary place?

▶ When you've spent time alone in the presence of God, how have you sensed him speaking to you?

▶ If you've never sensed God speaking to you what are other ways God gets your attention in "a gentle whisper"?

What the Bible Tells Us About Silence

Silence is the absence of noise and commotion. To "practice the discipline of silence" is to consciously withdraw from the ruckus of television, music, conversation, podcasts, social media, minor "emergencies" at work or home, etc. The discipline of silence is making the deliberate choice to enter into the quiet. Once there, instead of filling time and space with words, we listen attentively. We do so because as Solomon wisely noted, there is a "time to be quiet and a time to speak" (Ecclesiastes 3:7, NLT).

2. Consider these passages from the psalms and the prophets that emphasize the important role being quiet plays in the spiritual life.

▶ "Be still, and know that I am God. I will be exalted among the nations, I will be exalted in the earth!" (Psalm 46:10, ESV)

▶ "But I have calmed and quieted myself, I am like a weaned child with its mother; like a weaned child I am content." (Psalm 131:2)

▶ "But the LORD is in his holy temple; let all the earth keep silence before him." (Habakkuk 2:20, ESV)

▶ "The LORD is good to those whose hope is in him, to the one who seeks him; it is good to wait quietly for the salvation of the LORD. It is good for a man to bear the yoke while he is young. Let him sit alone in silence, for the LORD has laid it on him. Let him bury his face in the dust—there may yet be hope" (Lamentations 3:25–29).

Take five minutes to sit quietly with these verses. Slowly, carefully, simply read them several times. Let God's Word wash over you. Listen attentively. When you are done, journal some thoughts on a separate piece of paper.

Discussion Questions

▶ How can noise, talking, and busyness actually be addictive?

▶ How can you stop instinctively turning on the television when you walk in the house, or turning on your radio when you get in your car?

▶ How difficult would it be for you to go a half-day without speaking, or without immersing yourself in music and noise?

▶ Do you think there might be occasions when it's appropriate to withdraw even from written words? Can a person?

▶ What does sitting in silence make you feel? Can you name it?

3. Multiple times in the gospels, Jesus uttered the odd catchphrase "Whoever has ears, let them hear" (Matthew 11:15). What do you think he meant? Why is listening such a big deal in spirituality?

_____

_____

_____

_____

_____

_____

_____

Cultivating the Habits of Solitude and Silence

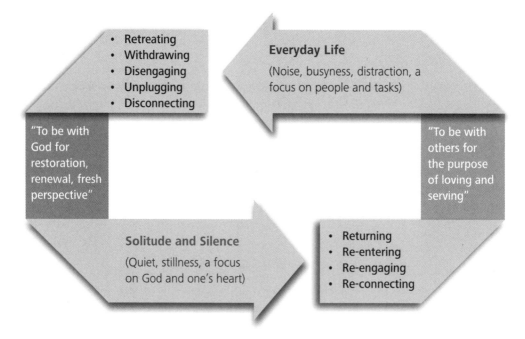

Take-Home Reflections

Here are some simple, everyday ways to build the rhythm of healthy disengagement and reengagement into our lives:

▷ Instead of staying glued to your smart phone all day, every day, put it away for short periods of time. See if you can go an hour without it, then try to go two, and then three.

▷ Set aside your "to do" list. Don't judge your worth to God on the basis of how much you accomplish.

▷ Turn off your electronics. Protect your time with God from others' demands.

▷ Resist the urge to immediately turn on the radio when you get in your car. Instead, use drive time to quietly meditate on a Bible verse.

▷ Sharpen your listening skills. Ask someone you're close to questions and really focus on their responses.

▷ Spend an evening with no television, YouTube, Netflix, etc.

▷ Set your alarm clock fifteen minutes earlier. Use that time to quietly read and contemplate Scripture.

▷ Find a solitary place and pray as the young prophet Samuel did, "Speak, LORD, for your servant is listening" (1 Samuel 3:9).

▷ Practice slipping away and being alone. If thirty minutes makes you uncomfortable, start with ten.

▷ Especially if you live in the city, devote a Saturday morning or Sunday afternoon to walking in the woods or countryside, or sitting in a quiet park.

▷ Take a break from podcasts and online sermons. Instead, sit quietly with your Bible, letting God's Word and Spirit speak to your soul.

▷ Declare a 24-hour electronics fast—no gadgets, gizmos, Internet, or cable.

Carve out time with God, simply sitting together quietly and enjoying each other's presence. No words are necessary.

Life Application

An important part of discipleship is learning how to apply God's truths to your life. Below are just a few ways you can start thinking about what you've learned and apply it to your daily life.

1. Memorize this topic's verse, Isaiah 30:15.

2. Read *The Practice of the Presence of God* by Brother Lawrence. This quick read tells of a seventeenth-century French monk's attempt to maintain a quiet awareness of God at all times.

3. Set aside fifteen minutes away from distractions. Pick a Bible verse about trust (Prov. 3:5–6), hope (Psalm 31:24), or resting in God (Psalm 62:5–6). Read it slowly to yourself, thinking about each phrase. Whenever other thoughts crowd in, repeat the verse in your mind.

Topic 4: Bible Reading & Study

Being Rooted in God's Truth

"Your word is a lamp for my feet,
a light on my path."
—Psalm 119:105

What can be said about the Bible that hasn't already been said? Its detractors call it names we can't repeat. Its fans call it everything from "the owner's manual for life," to "letters from home," to "the story of God."

Meanwhile, God's Word touts itself as an indispensable, life-saving, life-changing, life-enhancing revelation from God (2 Timothy 3:16–17; 2 Peter 1:20–21). To help us grasp all that, it likens itself to:

▶ *bread* (John 6:51)—necessary for life

▶ *gold* and *silver* (Psalm 12:6; 19:10)—making us spiritually wealthy beyond our wildest dreams

▶ a *fire* (Jeremiah 20:9; Luke 24:32)—uncontainable, able to consume what is dead

▶ a *hammer* (Jeremiah 23:29)—able to penetrate through hard heads and shatter hard hearts

▶ *honey* (Psalm 19:10)—delighting to our senses

▶ a *lamp* (Psalm 119:105)—lighting our way in a world that has been darkened by sin and evil

▶ *meat* (Hebrews 5:12–14)—able to sustain and nourish mature believers with profound truth

▶ *milk* (1 Peter 2:2)—full of simple truths to help "baby believers" grow

▶ a *mirror* (James 1:23–25)—able to show us what we truly look like inside and out

▶ *seed* (Matthew 13:18–23)—able to grow and bear fruit when it takes root in our lives

▶ a *sword* (Ephesians 6:17; Hebrews 4:12)—our best weapon in fighting spiritual battles

▶ *water* (Ephesians 5:25–27)—able to wash us and make us pure

As the diagram on the next page shows, we are to let God's Word take root in our lives, and then let it bear fruit.

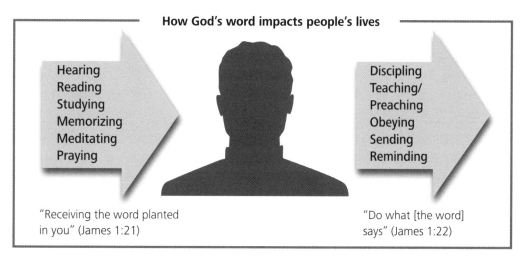

How God's word impacts people's lives

Hearing
Reading
Studying
Memorizing
Meditating
Praying

Discipling
Teaching/
Preaching
Obeying
Sending
Reminding

"Receiving the word planted
in you" (James 1:21)

"Do what [the word]
says" (James 1:22)

Here, we just want to focus on the truth that disciples of Jesus make Bible reading and study a regular practice. They want to hear God speak. They want to know his heart and do his will. A disciple is a student and practitioner of God's Word.

Bible Study

Reading the Bible

Reading is one of the fundamental ways we process information and acquire knowledge. Consider the Bible passages in the table that starts below. They emphasize the importance of reading God's Word.

Example	Scripture
God's command to Israel's future kings, that they must be immersed in divine truth.	"He must always keep that copy with him and read it daily as long as he lives. That way he will learn to fear the Lord his God by obeying all the terms of these instructions and decrees." (Deuteronomy 17:19, NLT)
Ezra the priest's plan for helping his countrymen grow in their faith after the exile.	"They remained standing in place for three hours while the Book of the Law of the LORD their God was read aloud to them. Then for three more hours they confessed their sins and worshiped the Lord their God." (Nehemiah 9:3, NLT)
The Apostle Paul's command to Timothy, a young pastor and Paul's protégé.	"Until I come, give attention to the public reading of Scripture, to exhortation and teaching." (1 Timothy 4:13, NASB)

1. What stands out to you from these examples?

_____

_____

2. What are your own habits of Bible reading?

3. If you are not a regular Bible reader, why? What holds you back?

Seven Ways to Read God's Word

▶ **Prayerfully** Before you begin, ask God to speak. Ask him for "ears to hear."

▶ **Expectantly** Believe that God wants to speak to you, even more than you want to hear from him. Then be alert for his voice.

▶ **Devotionally** See your Bible reading as a personal time *with* God rather than an assignment in trying to learn new information *about* God.

> "Read it through; pray it in; live it out; pass it on."—George Gritter

▶ **Slowly** Don't be in a rush. It's not a race. You don't get a prize for finishing your reading quickly. Linger. Savor the words. Re-read them.

▶ **Comprehensively** You wouldn't buy a best-selling novel (or a work of non-fiction), let it fall open to page 134, and start reading there. Or only read the final four chapters. Why do we do that with the Bible? Resist the urge to read randomly. Read through a book at a time. (You might consider starting with the Gospels: Matthew, Mark, Luke, and John.) Don't ignore big sections of Scripture. Consider reading the entire Bible cover to cover. That's the best way to get the truest sense of who God is, and what his story is about.

▶ **Regularly** Exercising once every three weeks is better than nothing. But such a sporadic training regimen isn't likely to get you in great physical condition. In the same way, occasional Bible reading isn't the optimal way to cultivate your relationship with God or prepare for helping others know God.

▶ **Obediently** Always read with a mindset of "I will do whatever God commands."

Studying the Bible

Bible study is the practice of a disciple of Jesus in which we try to deepen our understanding of God's Word so that we can more closely align our lives to what God has revealed and commanded.

4. What intimidates you most about studying the Bible?

_____

_____

_____

Bible study is engaging one's mind, heart, and will in order to understand and apply God's Word to everyday life.

There are all kinds of ways to approach Bible study. One of the simplest, clearest, and easiest methods is the three-step method that includes

Step #1: **Observing God's Word**

Step #2: **Interpreting God's Word**

Step #3: **Applying God's Word**

Below is a chart that shows the differences between these three phases of Bible study.

Observation	Interpretation	Application
"Open my eyes that I may see wonderful things in your law." (Psalm 119:18)	"Make me understand the way of your precepts, and I will meditate on your wondrous works." (Psalm 119:27, ESV)	"I will hurry, without delay, to obey your commands." (Psalm 119:60, NLT)
Asking: What does it say?	Asking: What does it mean?	Asking: What do I need to do?
Probing	Pondering	Practicing
Exploring	Explaining	Exercising
Discovering	Digesting	Doing
Seeing	Understanding	Obeying

Sample Bible Study

Let's look at those components in more detail, by actually doing a simple Bible study of Mark 8:22–26 together. Here's the passage:

> They came to Bethsaida, and some people brought a blind man and begged Jesus to touch him. He took the blind man by the hand and led him outside the village. When he had spit on the man's eyes and put his hands on him, Jesus asked, "Do you see anything?"
>
> He looked up and said, "I see people; they look like trees walking around."
>
> Once more Jesus put his hands on the man's eyes. Then his eyes were opened, his sight was restored, and he saw everything clearly. Jesus sent him home, saying, "Don't even go into the village."

Step #1: Observing God's Word

▶ **Pray** Ask the Spirit of God to be your teacher and to guide you into truth. Ask God for "eyes to see."

▶ **Read** Don't skim the passage the way you'd click and scroll through the Internet looking for something to catch your eye. Study the scene like a detective. What do you see? Noticing details requires conscious effort. Read the passage a second and third time. Don't read things "into" the text, but do try to draw out every relevant detail "from" the text.

▶ **Question** Dedicated Bible students bombard the text with questions. Study the chart below to discover some examples of questions you are encouraged to ask as you read the Scriptures.

▶ **Write** Record all your observations. Don't lose those "Aha!" insights by trusting them solely to your memory. Jot them down.

WHO?	Who is mentioned or involved here?
	Who seems to be the primary character?
WHAT?	What is going on or what is being said?
	What is the context for these events?
	What happened just before this?
	What is the sequence of events?
	What words (verbs, adjectives, prepositions, etc.) did the Spirit-guided author choose?
	What descriptive details do I see?
	What is the mood and setting?

WHEN?	When is this action taking place?
	When one character says or does _____, then . . .
WHERE?	Where are these events happening?
WHY?	Does the author explain why these events are unfolding?
	Does the author offer a motive for a character's words or actions?
HOW?	How do the characters respond?
	How does the scene conclude?

5. Take a few minutes to observe Mark 8:22–26. Jot down some of your observations:

_____

_____

_____

a. Why is it important to first objectively gather data before you do anything else?

_____

_____

_____

b. How solid will our interpretations of a passage be if we don't first carefully observe the passage? Why?

_____

_____

_____

Step #2: Interpreting God's Word

Once you've done the hard work of gathering facts—objectively asking what does it say and/or what do I see?—it's time to begin asking what does all this mean?

6. Suppose a friend studying Mark 8:22–26 with you said the following were things that were meaningful in the passage:

▶ Apart from the intercession and intervention of others, sick people will never experience Jesus' healing touch (v. 22).

▶ People aren't healed until they first agree to take Jesus' hand and follow him (v. 23).

▶ Spitting on people with disabilities helps them find healing (v. 24).

▶ When it comes to healing broken people, Jesus works in unique and unexpected ways (vss. 23–25).

▶ Divine healing is not always instantaneous (vss. 24–25).

▶ When Jesus takes us out of a bad situation and changes us, he does not want us going back into that same situation (vss. 23, 26).

Do you agree with any or all of those interpretations? Why or why not?

Knowing the Author's Intent

Imagine a terminally ill billionaire has drawn up her last will and testament.

After her funeral, when the will is read by a probate court, what's the goal? Is it to discover and do what she actually intended, or is it to have family factions interpret her words in five very different ways and bicker over the matter for the next twenty years?

Obviously the goal of a good attorney and a non-biased judge is to disregard what all the readers of the will want it to mean, and, instead, to discern and carry out the intent of the author of the will.

And so it is with interpreting God's Words. His intent must be our goal.

Scholars call the science of interpretation *hermeneutics*. As with all disciplines, there are agreed-upon principles and rules to follow. Disregarding these practices can lead to unbiblical ideas and the formation of pseudo-Christian cults. Finding out how various Bible scholars who've studied the language and culture of the Bible interpret a text is valuable.

In interpreting a passage, we are asking what does God intend to communicate here? We are not asking "What do I *feel* this passage means to me?"

Avoiding Wrong Bible Interpretations

Leave our presuppositions behind.

We must beware of trying to force a passage to fit with our preexisting beliefs or experiences. Disciples should always base their beliefs on what the Bible says rather than interpreting the Bible in accordance with their beliefs.

Resist getting overly creative.

It's tempting to look for some mysterious, hidden, symbolic meaning that no one has ever seen before. It's also dangerous.

Take into account historical, cultural, grammatical, and literary realities.

Though it's one timeless story, God's Word is comprised of a variety of kinds of literature. Plus it was compiled over 2,000 years in various Near Eastern and Mid-Eastern cultural settings by some forty different human authors writing in three languages—Hebrew, Aramaic, and Greek. If we insist on reading it through twenty-first century western eyes, we will misunderstand its meaning. This requires that you . . .

Ask and answer a LOT of questions!	For example: ▸ What kind of literature is this? Poetry? History? Prophecy? Wisdom? Epistolary? ▸ Is this passage narrative (a story) or didactic (instruction)? ▸ Is this text descriptive (simply telling about things that happened in a unique setting) or prescriptive (showing what should happen in all places at all times)?
Use the whole of Scripture to help interpret the parts of Scripture.	If other passages do not corroborate your interpretation of a text, you may be on dangerous ground. We should always use clear passages to help us grasp the meanings of unclear ones. Regarding the Mark 8 passage, since there are no other healings recorded in the gospels which show Jesus laying his hands on a person a second time, we are probably wise not to read too much into this unique event. In fact, that may be a valid interpretation: Jesus deals with each person uniquely.
Consider the context of a statement or passage.	For example, to understand Jesus' command to the healed man, "Don't go into the village," we need to look at comparable passages in Mark's gospel (1:44; 5:19, 43; see also Matthew 8:4 and 16:20).
Consult trustworthy commentaries on Scripture.	Seeing how Bible scholars interpret a text is a valuable help in understanding God's Word. So make use of Bible commentaries and study Bibles with notes from scholars.

7. Based on these rules of interpreting Scripture, what do you think of the "friend's" interpretations of Mark 8: 22–26 above?

_____

_____

_____

   a. What would you suggest as the meaning/interpretation of the story in Mark 8:22–26?

_____

_____

_____

Step #3: Applying God's Word

Applying the Bible is the final, crucial step of Bible study. This is where we put God's truth into practice. We live it out. We seek to be doers of the Word (James 1:22). Though a single verse or passage never has multiple interpretations (meanings), it can and does have a myriad of different possible applications.

For example, a men's group studying Ephesians 5:25 and the command to "love your wives, just as Christ loved the church" all agreed that the timeless *principle* there is that husbands are called to love their wives unconditionally and sacrificially. But their individual *applications* of that principle will look very different. For example,

- ▶ Bob has decided to back out of his fishing trip, and stay home to do three "honey do" projects that his wife Elizabeth has been begging him to do for months.

- ▶ Stephen feels nudged to apologize to his wife Ellen for being a slob and for not helping around the house. He wants to give her a weekend at a nice hotel.

How to Find Good Applications

After you have carefully observed a Bible passage and prayerfully determined what truth God meant to convey through it, you need to state that truth in the form of a broad "now" principle (like the guys did above). This serves as a kind of "bridge" between interpretation and application.

For example, in the case of our passage, Mark 8:22–26:

- ▶ **Observation** When some people brought a blind man to Jesus and requested he touch and heal the man, Jesus did so, in two phases.

- ▶ **Interpretation** Jesus demonstrated unique compassion and power to those who needed his touch.

8. What broad timeless principle do you see in this passage?

_____

_____

a. Finally, what **application(s)** do you get from the story of Jesus healing the blind man?

_____

_____

_____

Take-Home Reflections

The growing, fruitful disciple of Jesus makes it a practice to read and study God's Word. He or she has the attitude expressed by John Wesley:

"I want to know one thing—the way to heaven; how to land safe on that happy shore. God Himself has condescended to teach the way: For this very end he came from heaven. He hath written it down in a book. O give me that book! At any price, give me the book of God! I have it: Here is knowledge enough for me. Let me be a man of one book."

D. L. Moody on Why and How to Study the Bible

▶ "Someone has said that there are four things necessary in studying the Bible: Admit, submit, commit and transmit."

▶ "What we need as Christians is to be able to feed ourselves. How many there are who sit helpless and listless, with open mouths, hungry for spiritual things, and the minister has to try to feed them, while the Bible is a feast prepared, into which they never venture."

▶ "Depend upon it, my friends, if you get tired of the Word of God, and it becomes wearisome to you, you are out of communion with Him."

▶ "The more you love the Scriptures, the firmer will be your faith. There is little backsliding when people love the Scriptures."

Classic Bible Study Application Questions:

- Is there an overt command here to obey?
- Is there a promise to claim?
- Is there a new truth about God in which I can trust?
- Is there a sin to avoid?
- Is there a behavior to renounce?
- Is there an attitude to embrace?
- Is there an example to follow?
- Is there a prayer to express?

▶ "Bear in mind there is no situation in life for which you cannot find some word of consolation in Scripture."

▶ "The best law for Bible study is the law of perseverance."

▶ "So few grow, because so few study."

▶ "When I pray, I talk to God, but when I read the Bible, God is talking to me; and it is really more important that God should speak to me than that I should speak to Him. I believe we should know better how to pray if we knew our Bibles better. What is an army good for if they don't know how to use their weapons?"

▶ "I thank God there is a height in [the Bible] I do not know anything about, a depth I have never been able to fathom, and it makes the Book all the more fascinating."

Life Application

An important part of discipleship is learning how to apply God's truths to your life. Below are just a few ways you can start thinking about what you've learned and apply it to your daily life.

1. Memorize our memory verse, Psalm 119:105.

   "Your word is a lamp for my feet, a light on my path."

2. Review "D. L. Moody on Why and How to Study the Bible" on the previous page. Which of the individual points represent something you already do? Which represent something you would like to do? Determine which of the "want to" points you will immediately incorporate into your Bible study practices.

3. Read the following article about "Scripture Memory."

Scripture Memory

A lot of people (especially people who are upwards of 30 years old) are inclined to think *I can't memorize a bunch of Bible verses!*

Not true! Think of all the information, all the facts you've already got stored in your mind—computer passwords, pin numbers, funny lines from movies, phone numbers, important dates (like your anniversary—right, guys?), addresses, etc. And that doesn't include all the song lyrics you know by heart.

The truth is we *can* memorize Scripture. The only question is *will* we?

Why does Scripture memory matter?

Internalizing God's truth is life-changing! It:

- Gives us victory over sin. Psalm 119:11 says that when we hide God's Word in our hearts, it is a great defense against temptation. Jesus proved this in his own wilderness struggle against the devil (Matthew 4:1–11).

- Radically affects our lives by helping renew our minds (Romans 12:1–2).

- Helps us overcome worry; God promises to flood our lives with peace when our minds are fixed on him and his Word (Isaiah 26:3; Philippians 4:6–8).

- Gives us confidence when we share our faith (1 Peter 3:15). No longer will we feel tongue-tied or wonder what to say in a conversation about spiritual matters.

When is the best time to memorize?

Most people find the best times are probably just before going to bed, or when you first wake up in the morning. But it may be that your mind is sharpest at 2:15 in the afternoon, or around lunchtime. The point is, there is no "right" time. Just do it whenever you can really focus and concentrate. NOTE: Some people like to memorize while running or walking *(Warning! You can twist an ankle doing it this way!).*

How much Scripture should I memorize?

Don't get too ambitious and try to memorize all four gospels the first week (at least not in Greek). Shoot for one or two verses per week, and keep reviewing them until you really have them down.

What is the "trick"?

Now we get down to the nitty-gritty. Here are some tips for getting God's Word into your mind and heart:

▶ Pick out the verse you intend to memorize.

▶ Read the chapter that contains the verse so that you understand the context—what's going on in the background.

▶ Include the reference (for example, Psalm 119:105) as part of the verse. Say this *before* reading the verse and again *after* you've finished. This is important because it helps you remember exactly where the verse is located. Then you won't get in situations where you end up saying, "Well, I don't remember where that verse is, but I know it's in the Bible *somewhere*."

▶ Read the verse several times out loud. This gives you the flow of the verse.

▶ Break the verse into chunks, memorizing phrase by phrase. Say the reference by itself. Then the reference and the first "chunk." Then the reference, the first, and the second part of the verse. And so forth, until you've said the reference, the whole verse, and the reference again.

▶ Carefully write the verse on an index card, note pad, or in your mobile phone, thinking about it as you go. This helps cement it in your mind. For visual learners, writing the verse works better than merely saying it over and over. Once you've written the verse down, take it with you everywhere you go and . . .

▶ Review your pants off! (Not *literally*, of course, but several times each day during the next two or three days).

That's all there is to it. Isn't that simple?

A final reminder

God will help you as you memorize. He wants his Word to take root and bear fruit in your life even more than you do. (See Deuteronomy 6:6 and Colossians 3:16.)

You can count on his help!

Topic 5: Prayer

Communing with God

> "Pray in the Spirit on all occasions with all kinds of prayers and requests. With this in mind, be alert and always keep on praying for all the Lord's people."
> —Ephesians 6:18

What if you had a friendship with someone you could call any time, night or day? A friend who met with you regularly and allowed you to talk non-stop for ten, twenty, thirty minutes—or more—and never asked you to stop? Or maybe you just send out a quick call or text now and then, and no matter what, that friend was always there to answer. Suppose as well that this friend reached out to you to give you guidance, support, love, and encouragement—even when you didn't call and ask for it first.

You would feel deeply loved by that friend, right? Happily, that's a description of how any of Christ's followers can approach God.

In this lesson, we're going to see that disciples of Jesus imitate Jesus in the way he prayed.

> "Pray until you can pray; pray to be helped to pray and do not give up praying because you cannot pray. For ... when you think you cannot pray that is when you are praying."
> —Charles Spurgeon

Bible Study

What Is Prayer?

In its purest essence, prayer is simply communing with the One (see Exodus 33:11) who is nearer to us than we realize (Acts 17:28). Biblical prayer can be silence or it can be an ongoing dialogue with God (1 Thessalonians 5:17). It's less a way to get stuff, and more a way to draw close to the Father in heaven.

1. How have you experienced praying to God?

_____

_____

_____

_____

Why do we pray?

Prayer is a mystery. God is *all-knowing*. We can't tell him things he doesn't already know. And he is *sovereign*—working and weaving everything everywhere together to accomplish his perfect eternal purposes. These truths make us ask: Why do I even need to pray?

And yet, for reasons we can't fully understand, *God commands us to pray*: "Devote yourselves to prayer, being watchful and thankful" (Colossians 4:2). Furthermore, God tells us that *our prayers are eternally significant*: "Confess your sins to each other and pray for each other so that you may be healed. The earnest prayer of a righteous person has great power and produces wonderful results" (James 5:16, NLT).

2. What results have you seen from praying?

_____

_____

_____

The following list surely isn't exhaustive. But here are a few reasons prayer is so essential to followers of Jesus.

Prayer is how we approach God.

"Draw near to God and He will draw near to you" (James 4:8, NASB). Never forget that God longs for a relationship with us. Proverbs 15:8 tells us, "The LORD . . . delights in the prayers of the upright" (NLT). Even if we don't know what to say, God's Spirit prays for us (Romans 8:26). When we approach God with respect, we need not worry about praying wrong.

Prayer aligns us with God's purposes for our lives.

If we are wise, we recognize that God, being good and loving, desires our best. Consequently, a big part of prayer is learning to relinquish our desires and say "your will be done" (Matthew 6:10). As C. S. Lewis said, "If God had granted all the silly prayers I've made in my life, where would I be now?"[1] In another place Lewis said, "Prayer doesn't change God, it changes me."

Prayer is an expression of faith.

"Without faith it is impossible to please God, because anyone who comes to him must believe that he exists and that he rewards those who earnestly seek him" (Hebrews 11:6). Behind all true prayer is a belief that there is one who is there, one who hears; in all true prayer, there is an admission of "you are the One I need; you are the One who can help; you are the One I trust."

Prayer gives peace.

"Do not be anxious about anything, but in everything by prayer and supplication with thanksgiving let your requests be made known to God. And the peace of God, which surpasses all understanding, will guard your hearts and your minds in Christ Jesus" (Philippians 4:6–7, ESV).

Prayer is powerful.

Though we don't understand exactly how prayer works—only that it isn't a magic formula or guarantee—there are plenty of examples in Scripture and in more recent history of *prayer making a difference.* For instance, when Hezekiah was dying, he prayed and wept. God heard and told the prophet Isaiah: "Go and tell Hezekiah, 'This is what the LORD, the God of your father David, says: I have heard your prayer and seen your tears; I will add fifteen years to your life'" (Isaiah 38:5).

Prayer changes things—at the very least it changes us.

"In the name of Jesus, amen"

Praying "in the name of Jesus" means more than mindlessly tacking that phrase on to the ends of our prayers. Biblically, a name represents all that a person is and stands for. Doing anything in a person's name means to do that thing as if he or she were doing it. To pray in Jesus' name means praying the kind of prayers Jesus would pray. An "in the name of Christ" prayer should reflect who Jesus is—his person and works.

---

1 C. S. Lewis, *Letters to Malcolm: Chiefly on Prayer* (Fort Washington, PA: Harvest Books, 1973): 28

3. What specific factors motivate you to pray?

_____

_____

_____

As with any close relationship, prayer needs to be more than, "Can you give me this? And that? And that?" A running conversation with the Almighty should include the same kinds of exchanges found in any intimate relationship:

▶ Expressions of appreciation and admiration

▶ Careful listening

▶ Revealed hopes and dreams

▶ Admissions of disappointment, frustration, and struggle.

Prayer is an ongoing, back-and-forth conversation that leads to intimacy with God.

How Should We Pray?

Take a few moments to carefully and thoughtfully read these verses that tell us *how* to pray:

In faith	"I tell you, you can pray for anything, and if you believe that you've received it, it will be yours" (Mark 11:24, NLT).
In the name of Jesus	"I will do whatever you ask in my name, so that the Father may be glorified in the Son" (John 14:13).
According to God's will	"This is the confidence we have in approaching God: that if we ask anything according to his will, he hears us. And if we know that he hears us—whatever we ask—we know that we have what we asked of him" (1 John 5:14–15).
Unceasingly	"Pray continually" (1 Thessalonians 5:17).
Confidently	"Therefore let us draw near with confidence to the throne of grace, so that we may receive mercy and find grace to help in time of need" (Hebrews 4:16, NASB).
Stubbornly	"Then Jesus told his disciples a parable to show them that they should always pray and not give up" (Luke 18:1).
With the help of the Spirit	"In the same way, the Spirit helps us in our weakness. We do not know what we ought to pray for, but the Spirit himself intercedes for us through wordless groans" (Romans 8:26).

Stop and think about this last point for a moment. The Spirit helps us to pray. This is a huge comfort. When we're clueless, he knows. When we can't, he can!

4. Based on these verses and truths, how would you evaluate your prayer life of late?

_____

_____

_____

5. The Bible gives some explicit warnings about how *not* to pray. What actions or attitudes cited in the following verses are clear hindrances to God-honoring prayer? Write your answer on the blank spaces in the chart.

Passage	What's the snare to God-pleasing prayer?
Luke 8:9–14	
Psalm 66:18–20	
James 4:2–3; 1 Peter 3:7	
Matthew 6:5–8	
James 1:5–7	
Isaiah 29:13	

Are there "rules" regarding the details of praying?

The short answer is no. In Scripture we see:

Prayers from all kinds of people:

▶ Children (1 Samuel 3:10)

▶ Elderly widows (Luke 2:36–38)

▶ Kings (Psalm 139)

▶ Frightened people (Jonah 1:14)

▶ Military leaders (Joshua 7:6–9)

▶ Broken adults (Judges 16:28)

People praying:

▶ Alone (Matthew 14:23)

▶ In groups (Acts 1:14)

People crying out to God:

▶ In bed (Psalm 63:6)

▶ On the beach (Acts 21:5)

▶ On mountainsides (Luke 6:12)

▶ Outdoors (Genesis 24:11–12)

▶ At the temple (Luke 18:10)

Time people prayed:

▶ Fixed-hour prayers (Psalm 55:17)

▶ Midnight prayers (Acts 16:25)

▶ Morning prayers (Psalm 5:3)

People praying while:

▶ Sitting (2 Samuel 7:18)

▶ Standing (Mark 11:25)

▶ Kneeling (Acts 9:40)

▶ Lifting hands toward heaven (1 Kings 8:22)

The Prayer Life of Jesus

- He prayed in the early morning (Mark 1:35).
- He prayed in the evening (Mark 6:46–47).
- He spent whole nights praying (Luke 6:12).
- He prayed in lonely places (Luke 5:16).
- He agonized in prayer (Luke 22:39–46).
- He died praying (Luke 23:46).
- He praised the Father in his prayers (Matthew 11:25).
- He thanked the Father in prayer (John 11:41).
- He prayed for the will of the Father (Matthew 26:39).
- He prayed for his followers (John 17:9).
- He prayed forgiveness for his enemies (Luke 23:34).
- He prayed for children (Matthew 19:13–15).
- He prayed for himself (John 17:1).

Believers praying:

▶ Silently (1 Samuel 1:13)

▶ In a loud voice (Ezra 3:11–13)

▶ With joy (Philippians 1:4)

Jesus prayed:

▶ Through tears (Hebrews 5:7)

▶ While looking up (John 11:41)

▶ With his face to the ground (Matthew 26:39)

Basically, there are no hard and fast rules to follow. What matters is engaging God. Giving him your attention. Talking to and communing with him—everywhere and all the time.

6. How do you like to pray—when, where, body posture, etc.?

_____

_____

_____

What should we pray about?

Jesus gave his followers some guidelines for prayer in Matthew 6:9–13—not a mantra to memorize and repeat mindlessly, but a short outline for conversing with God. Look at the parts of the so-called "Lord's Prayer:"

> "Some people think God does not like to be troubled with our constant coming and asking. The way to trouble God is not to come at all."—D. L. Moody

Statement or Request	Focus	Explanation
"Our Father in heaven . . .	God's nature	Our prayers are directed to a loving father who wants the best for his children and whose heart we can trust.
hallowed be your name . . .	God's glory	Our prayer should always focus on bringing honor and praise to God.
your kingdom come . . .	God's kingdom	Our prayers ought to seek the righteous rule of God in every part of life.
your will be done, on earth as it is in heaven . . .	God's will	Our prayers must always submit to the higher plan and wiser purposes of God.
Give us today our daily bread . . .	God's provision	Our prayers need to be humble and dependent, looking to God to meet our needs.
And forgive us our debts, as we also have forgiven our debtors . . .	God's mercy	Our prayers acknowledge our constant need to receive and dispense grace.
And lead us not into temptation, but deliver us from the evil one."	God's protection	Our prayers recognize the sobering reality of evil.

7. How could you apply Jesus' "Lord's Prayer" outline to your own life today?

_____

_____

_____

Take-Home Reflections

It's easy to get so preoccupied with "answers" to prayer, we forget that the goal is communing with God. Inherent in all prayer is an acknowledgement of God. Permeating all prayer should be an enjoyment of God. Prayer is trusting that God knows what is best for us, even if we can't see it.

Prayer is lingering in the divine presence. It can be wordless. The point is to pay attention to God. Draw near. When you get right down to it, he is our hearts' truest, deepest desire, not some lesser blessing he can provide.

Go ahead and offer up prayers for needs and "stuff." But remember: even if God's response is "Wait" or "Not yet" or even "No," the biggest blessing is that you are getting to spend time with your Creator!

> "In prayer it is better to have a heart without words than words without a heart."—John Bunyan

Think of it as a gift when God answers in a way you don't expect or even desire. It means you get to respond to God's response. If his answer is "no," you can, by faith, thank God for wisely and lovingly protecting you from something hurtful or detrimental that you can't see. If the outcome is still pending, you can bring the subject up again at a later date (Luke 18:1–8). If God gives you what you seek, you get to come back and express thanksgiving and gratitude.

The lesson in all this? God offers you marvelous gifts through prayer. But don't settle for mere gifts when the Giver also offers you himself. Focus on the Giver, not the gift.

Life Application

An important part of discipleship is learning how to apply God's truths to your life. Below are just a few ways you can start thinking about what you've learned and apply it to your daily life.

1. Memorize our memory verse, Ephesians 6:18.

   "Pray in the Spirit on all occasions with all kinds of prayers and requests. With this in mind, be alert and always keep on praying for all the saints."

2. Read Paul's prayers in Ephesians 1:15–23 and 3:14–21.

3. Ask your group, spouse, or a friend to work through the exercise on the following page with you.

> "The main lesson about prayer is this: Do it! Do it! Do it! You want to be taught to pray? My answer is: pray."—John Laidlaw

Pray Honestly and Boldly

One great thing about group prayer times is that they give us an opportunity to pray specifically and boldly about the real issues going on here and now, in our own lives. Use the sample prayer requests below to spark or broaden your thinking, and to help *focus* your own prayer requests.

Sample Prayer Requests

▶ I need more joy in my life. Would you pray that I could recapture a sense of spiritual awe and delight?

▶ My spiritual life is kind of blah. Please pray that I'll recapture my desire to live for God.

▶ I have a family member or friend who needs Christ. Pray that God will use me to reach him/her. Pray that I'll be sensitive and available.

▶ I'm realizing there are certain areas of my life that I need to surrender (or re-surrender) to God. I'm struggling! Please pray that I'll take this step.

▶ There's an unresolved conflict that is affecting one of my primary relationships. Pray that I'll do right—do everything within my power this week to begin to address it and fix it.

▶ I'm facing a big, life-decision. I sure could use wisdom.

▶ Lately, I haven't been taking care of my heart or making my relationship with Christ my top priority (Proverbs 4:23). Pray that I'll exercise the discipline to live more like Mary and less like Martha (Luke 10:38-42).

▶ I keep tripping over the same temptation(s). Pray that I will lean on God's strength this week to say "NO!"

▶ I need more boldness in my faith.

▶ I'm discouraged about _____. Pray that I will bounce back.

▶ I feel like I'm under attack. Pray that I'll be alert and wise.

▶ Pray that I have courage to invite _____ to church or my small group.

▶ I don't feel right now like I know God very well. Pray that he'll reveal himself to me and that I'll have eyes of faith to see and ears to hear what he's saying to me.

▶ Our/my finances are not in the greatest shape. Pray that God would show what needs to be done.

▶ I feel far away from God. Pray that I'll make my way back.

▶ Pray that I'll have the courage to look hard at my life and to identify wrong attitudes or actions. And that with God's help, I'll begin to make changes.

▶ My life feels chaotic and out-of-control. Would you pray that I'd find a healthier balance?

▶ Pray that I'd be the kind of spouse I need to be (loving, selfless, thoughtful, kind, etc.).

▶ Pray for me this week as a parent. I need strength/patience/gentleness/wisdom, etc.

▶ I'm anxious about _____. Pray that I'll experience God's perfect peace this week.

▶ I have an important relationship that needs some work. Pray that I will have supernatural wisdom to know what to do, the courage to do right, and that my actions will be rooted in love.

▶ I need to confront someone in love. Pray that I'll know what to say and how to say it.

▶ I feel guilty about _____. Pray that I can get to the bottom of this and resolve it.

▶ My faith is really weak and shaky. Pray that I'll keep clinging to God.

▶ I'm angry about _____. Pray that I'll process and deal with these things in a God-honoring way.

▶ I'm realizing I've buried some old hurts and wounds and it's affecting my life and relationships. Would you pray that I can deal healthily with these things and move forward?

▶ I need to ask forgiveness from someone I've wronged. Pray for the grace and courage to do this ASAP.

▶ I'm going through some trials just now—pray that I'll respond in a mature way—that I'll *grow* and not *grumble*.

▶ I pray you would heal _____. Give me the strength to help this person. If it is not your will to heal now, please give us all comfort, courage, and peace as we walk through this tough time.

If you don't know what kinds of things to pray for, let this spark your thinking. If you're reluctant to open up, take a risk. Alfred Lord Tennyson said it best: "More things are wrought by prayer than this world dreams of."

Topic 6: Fasting

Cultivating an Appetite for the Things of God

> "'Even now,' declares the LORD, 'return to
> me with all your heart, with fasting and
> weeping and mourning.'"
> —Joel 2:12

Maybe you've heard spiritually minded people speak about *fasting*. Or perhaps you've got friends who have given up certain foods or habits for Lent. What's all that about? And more importantly, why is fasting such an important practice for the disciples of Jesus?

In this lesson, we want to examine this obscure, often misunderstood practice.

▶ What is it?

▶ Why is it important?

▶ How do we practice it?

When you hear the word "fasting," what thoughts and images come to mind?

_____

_____

_____

What is fasting?

The Old Testament Hebrew verb "to fast" is *tsoom*. It means, as we might expect, to abstain from food. The comparable New Testament Greek word is *nēsteuō*. This word has the added nuance of meaning "to be empty."

Biblical fasting, then, as defined by most people, is choosing to go without food—and sometimes drink—for a specified length of time. There are other types of fasts, but we'll start with food.

Bible Study

1. What's the longest time you ever went without eating? What were the reasons?

_____

_____

_____

Why Is Fasting Important?

The Bible seems to set forth at least four purposes for fasting.

Purpose #1: **To show sorrow for sin, whether personal or national.**

In the table below, read the verses in the right column, and in the left, write down who it is that is fasting to show sorrow for sin. Identify whether this is an example of personal or national sorrow.

Who is expressing sorrow?	Scripture
	"When they had assembled at Mizpah, they drew water and poured it out before the Lord. On that day they fasted and there they confessed, 'We have sinned against the Lord'" (1 Samuel 7:6).
	"So I turned to the Lord God and pleaded with him in prayer and petition, in fasting, and in sackcloth and ashes. I prayed to the Lord my God and confessed: 'Lord, the great and awesome God, who keeps his covenant of love with those who love him and keep his commandments, we have sinned and done wrong. We have been wicked and have rebelled; we have turned away from your commands and laws'" (Daniel 9:3–5).
	"Then Ezra withdrew from before the house of God and went to the chamber of Jehohanan the son of Eliashib, where he spent the night, neither eating bread nor drinking water, for he was mourning over the faithlessness of the exiles" (Ezra 10:6, ESV).
	"They said to me, 'Those who survived the exile and are back in the province are in great trouble and disgrace. The wall of Jerusalem is broken down, and its gates have been burned with fire.' When I heard these things, I sat down and wept. For some days I mourned and fasted and prayed before the God of heaven" (Nehemiah 1:3–4).

2. Why not just pray about sin? Why the added step of denying oneself food?

_____

_____

_____

_____

_____

Purpose #2: **To attempt to hear from God and/or to seek his intervention.**

Fasting can help us focus on seeking God and listening to hear his voice.

Circumstance	Scripture
When Esther was going to ask the Persian king to spare her fellow Jews.	"Go, gather all the Jews to be found in Susa, and hold a fast on my behalf, and do not eat or drink for three days, night or day. I and my young women will also fast as you do. Then I will go to the king, though it is against the law, and if I perish, I perish" (Esther 4:16, ESV).
Before the Jewish exiles began the trip back to their homeland.	"And there by the Ahava Canal, I gave orders for all of us to fast and humble ourselves before our God. We prayed that he would give us a safe journey and protect us, our children, and our goods as we traveled. For I was ashamed to ask the king for soldiers and horsemen to accompany us and protect us from enemies along the way. After all, we had told the king, 'Our God's hand of protection is on all who worship him, but his fierce anger rages against those who abandon him.' So we fasted and earnestly prayed that our God would take care of us, and he heard our prayer" (Ezra 8:21–23, NLT).

3. Imagine you had a friend who said, "Fasting seems like you're just trying to manipulate God—_Look at how serious I am—I'm not even eating! Now, God, you have to give me what I'm asking for!_" How would you respond to this friend?

_____

_____

_____

_____

Purpose #3: **To seek discernment for a looming decision or guidance for next steps.**

Circumstance	Scripture
Paul, immediately after his conversion.	"He remained there blind for three days and did not eat or drink" (Acts 9:9, NLT).
The church, before sending out missionaries.	"Now in the church at Antioch there were prophets and teachers: Barnabas, Simeon called Niger, Lucius of Cyrene, Manaen (who had been brought up with Herod the tetrarch) and Saul. While they were worshiping the Lord and fasting, the Holy Spirit said, 'Set apart for me Barnabas and Saul for the work to which I have called them.' So after they had fasted and prayed, they placed their hands on them and sent them off" (Acts 13:1–3).
Paul and his cohorts, before appointing and commissioning church leaders.	"They preached the gospel in that city and won a large number of disciples. Then they returned to Lystra, Iconium and Antioch, strengthening the disciples and encouraging them to remain true to the faith. 'We must go through many hardships to enter the kingdom of God,' they said. Paul and Barnabas appointed elders for them in each church and, with prayer and fasting, committed them to the Lord, in whom they had put their trust" (Acts 14:21–23).

4. How and why might fasting help you have clarity when you face big decisions?

_____

_____

_____

_____

Purpose #4: **To practice self-control.**

"For this very reason, make every effort to add to your faith goodness; and to goodness, knowledge; and to knowledge, self-control; and to self-control, perseverance; and to perseverance, godliness; and to godliness, mutual affection; and to mutual affection, love. For if you possess these qualities in increasing measure, they will keep you from being ineffective and unproductive in your knowledge of our Lord Jesus Christ" (2 Peter 1:5–8).

> "Fasting is abstaining from anything that hinders prayer."
> —Andrew Bonar

Remember the idea that the Greek word for fasting, *nēsteuō*, also means "to be empty"? This is why fasting is important to disciples of Jesus. Sometimes we "fill up" on the wrong things. We become so satiated with earthly things, we don't have appetite or room for the things of God.

> "Prayer is reaching out after the unseen; fasting is letting go of all that is seen and temporal. Fasting helps express, deepen, confirm the resolution that we are ready to sacrifice anything, even ourselves to attain what we seek for the kingdom of God."
> —Andrew Murray

When we choose to do without something to which we've grown accustomed, and perhaps even attached, we feel empty and needy. *And that's a good thing, not a bad thing!* The goal with fasting is to take our emptiness and our restless powerful longings to Jesus, who alone can satisfy. The point is to deprive ourselves, to exercise self-control over any and all powerful appetites so that we can focus more fully on God and cultivate our love for and trust in him.

What is something that would be hard for you to give up—even temporarily?

How Does Fasting "Work"?

In the Old Testament, only one fast a year was commanded—the Day of Atonement (Leviticus 16:29, 31; 23:27–32). Late in Jewish history, other fasts were instituted (Esther 9:31; Zechariah 8:19). All other

NOTE

Fasting is not a statement about God's good gifts. When we choose to abstain from food or sex or technology, we are not denigrating those things. Each, when viewed and used properly, is a wonderful blessing from God. Fasting is one way to help us make sure those good things don't become paramount things. Fasting helps us redirect our desires toward the only one who can truly satisfy us.

fasting was personal and/or voluntary. Since the Jewish people saw sunset as the end of the day, they would often eat supper just before sunset, then fast until supper after sunset the following day (thus skipping a breakfast and a lunch).

In the New Testament we don't find any explicit commands to fast. We note that Jesus fasted (Matthew 4:2) and he assumed his disciples would (Matthew 6:16–18; Luke 5:33–35). From the passages already given, we know that Paul participated in the spiritual practice of fasting.

> "Fasting, if we conceive of it truly, must not be confined to the question of food and drink; fasting should really be made to include abstinence from anything which is legitimate in and of itself for the sake of some special spiritual purpose. There are many bodily functions which are right and normal and perfectly legitimate, but which for special peculiar reasons in certain circumstances should be controlled. That is fasting."
> —Martyn Lloyd-Jones

5. What would be some good reasons for you to fast in your life right now?

_____

_____

_____

_____

_____

6. What would be some wrong reasons to fast?

_____

_____

_____

_____

_____

7. What's your biggest takeaway from this lesson?

_____

_____

_____

_____

_____

> "The purpose of fasting is to loosen to some degree the ties which bind us to the world of material things and our surroundings as a whole, in order that we may concentrate all our spiritual powers upon the unseen and eternal things."
> —O. Hallesby

Take-Home Reflections

Tips and Reminders for the Spiritual Discipline of Fasting

▶ If you have a chronic medical condition or are pregnant, check with your physician first.

▶ Drink plenty of water.

▶ Start small—instead of fasting for a day, fast for one meal.

▶ Consider fasting from a particular kind of food to which you feel unhealthily attached, such as desserts or caffeine.

▶ Remember that fasting from things we *want*—such as entertainment—can sometimes be harder than things we really *need*—like food.

▶ Remember fasting isn't magic, and it doesn't obligate God to give you what you seek (2 Samuel 12:16–20).

▶ Use missed meal times—prep, cooking, eating, and clean-up—as opportunities to draw near to God and pray.

▶ Don't be legalistic. If not drinking coffee gives you a splitting headache, then drink your morning java!

▶ Don't make a public declaration of your fasting (Matthew 6:16–18).

▶ Don't limit fasting to food. You may abstain from shopping, the Internet, social media, excessive exercise, going to movies, email, watching sports, even sex with your spouse for a brief time (1 Corinthians 7:5).

▶ Break your fast carefully. Don't gorge on whatever you've been fasting from.

Life Application

An important part of discipleship is learning how to apply God's truths to your life. Below are just a few ways you can start thinking about what you've learned and apply it to your daily life.

1. Memorize our memory verse, Joel 2:12.

2. Read and consider Isaiah 58:6–7.

3. Wrestle with one or two of the following:

▶ Does the thought of doing without certain things—even temporarily— make you fidgety or nervous?

▶ What things do you turn to when you begin to feel restless or empty?

▶ What "wants" in your life would you find most difficult to deny yourself?

▶ The purpose of fasting, or abstaining from a thing, is to loosen that thing's grip on your soul. Fasting is an external practice meant to restore or foster internal health. Agree or not? Why?

▶ When it comes to you personally, would fasting from food be the best way to restore or foster internal health? Or would another form of fasting be more effective? Why?

Understanding Generosity and Stewardship

"Remember this: Whoever sows sparingly
will also reap sparingly, and whoever sows
generously will also reap generously. Each of you
should give what you have decided in your heart
to give, not reluctantly or under compulsion, for
God loves a cheerful giver."

—2 Corinthians 9:6–7

A Parable

In 1980 two brothers received a large inheritance from their father's estate. One son took his $150,000 and went on a lavish spending spree. He bought himself a sports car, a ski boat, and assorted other gadgets and toys. He took exotic trips. In eighteen short months, his money was gone.

> How we handle money speaks volumes about what and who we really believe.

The other son took his money and decided to invest it. He did some research, and then used half his windfall to buy stock in two "up-and-coming" companies. Maybe you've heard of them: a software company called Microsoft? A computer company named Apple? With the other half of his unexpected blessing he created a foundation that has built schools in India and drilled water wells in Africa.

Both brothers were given a great gift, but only one was wise. One brother, in his short-sighted selfishness, blessed a car dealer, a ski boat salesman, and some hotel owners. There's no telling how many thousands of lives the other brother is continuing to bless with his visionary generosity.

You may not know that Jesus talked more about money than He did about heaven and hell combined! Meaning, we *have* to study this subject. If we avoid it, we ignore a major discipleship issue.

Perhaps money has never been an issue for you . . . you're rolling in the dough . . . you have a big closet in your house full of cash and you're like a broken ATM when it comes to helping others.

More likely, as with most people, money is an ongoing stressor in your life. Whether it's:

▶ Saving, "Yeah, right!"

▶ Spending, "Somebody stop me!"

▶ Investing, "Who are you kidding?!"

▶ Borrowing, "I'm in debt up to my eyeballs!"

▶ Giving, "Sorry, there's nothing left to give!"

> "If you have something you can't give away, perhaps you don't own it. Maybe it owns you?"
> —Howard Hendricks

Just the mention of this topic leaves most people feeling uncomfortable or discouraged.

This is a lesson about money, and about cultivating the wise and joyous habit of being generous and making a difference with our finances.

Bible Study

1. Why do you think this subject of money causes such tension within people? Why such awkwardness between people?

_____

_____

_____

_____

Three Encouraging Truths About Money:

Truth #1: God is generous with his children; he promises to provide for *all* of our needs.

2. Look up and read these verses: Psalm 145:16; Matthew 7:11; and Philippians 4:19. What strikes you most about these statements and promises?

_____

_____

_____

Truth #2: **God gives generously to his people so that we can give generously to others.**

This principle goes all the way back to the calling of Abraham. God promised to bless him, and then said "and you will be a blessing" (Genesis 12:2). In other words, don't hoard—give! Be a conduit of God's blessings, not a black hole.

3. Take a moment to read 2 Corinthians 9:6–11, the passage from which we get our memory verse for this topic. What does Paul mean when he uses the agricultural imagery of "sowing and reaping?"

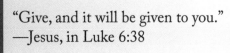

"Give, and it will be given to you."
—Jesus, in Luke 6:38

_____

_____

_____

_____

You don't have to be a farmer to realize that if you only plant a few seeds, you'll only get a small harvest. The more you put into the ground, the more you stand to receive back from the ground. This is also true in the spiritual realm. The blessings may not be financial, but there is a return.

Truth #3: **God says he blesses the generous.**

Did you happen to note all the promises of blessing in the passage you just read? God said that those who sow generously by giving generously to the work of God will:

▶ Have what they need to live (v. 8)

▶ See increasing fruit from their sacrificial contributions (vss. 8, 11)

▶ *Receive* more in order to be able to *give* more (v. 11)

A careful reading of the New Testament shows that the Lord calls his followers to selflessly and generously share with others the blessings that he has placed in their care. Disciples don't stockpile money and things—they share. They invest in eternal causes for the glory of God, for the good of others, and for their own spiritual well-being.

Let's look at an incident from Jesus' life and ministry that can help us get a grip on the subject of money—ironically, by showing us how to *loosen* our grip on it. Here's the scene:

"Jesus sat down opposite the place where the offerings were put and watched the crowd putting their money into the temple treasury. Many rich people threw in large amounts.

But a poor widow came and put in two very small copper coins, worth only a few cents.

"Calling his disciples to him, Jesus said, 'Truly I tell you, this poor widow has put more into the treasury than all the others. They all gave out of their wealth; but she, out of her poverty, put in everything—all she had to live on.'" (Mark 12:41–44)

4. What do you notice about this scene—what stands out to you?

_____

_____

_____

_____

A word of explanation: At the temple in Jerusalem, in the Court of the Women, were thirteen trumpet-shaped collection receptacles for receiving worshipers' offerings. Copper coins were the smallest Jewish coin in circulation. Two were equal to $1/64$ of what a common laborer would make in a day.

Notice the contrast that Jesus noticed:

Many Rich People	One Poor Widow
They gave large amounts.	She gave two very small copper coins.
They gave out of their surplus—literally, out of their excess, their leftovers.	She gave out of her poverty—literally, out of her need or lack. She gave everything she had, all that she had to live on.
They made contributions—granted, sizable ones.	She made a sacrifice.
Not particularly noteworthy to Jesus.	Remarkable to Jesus—"Come see this!"

Why does Jesus single out this obscure woman who gave such a paltry sum? What's his point? It's this:

Followers of Jesus honor God, bless others,
and find great reward in giving!

Cultivating a Generous Attitude

How can we cultivate this kind of attitude that leads us to give so generously? We have to do three things:

#1: **Recognize that "your" stuff is really not your stuff.**

Carefully read the following verses:

- ▶ "The whole earth is mine" (Exodus 19:5).

- ▶ "Everything under heaven belongs to me" (Job 41:11).

- ▶ "The earth is the LORD'S, and everything in it" (Psalm 24:1).

- ▶ "'The silver is mine and the gold is mine,' declares the LORD Almighty" (Haggai 2:8).

5. If God is the true owner of *everything*, what does that mean as far as "your" paycheck, possessions, property, portfolio, etc.?

_____

_____

_____

Do you see it? The Bible teaches that "our" stuff is not really our stuff. It all belongs to God. He's the owner of it all and we are simply caretakers, managers, or stewards—trustworthy servants (1 Peter 4:10; 1 Corinthians 4:2; 6:20).

6. How does this truth—understood and embraced—change the way you look at your spending decisions?

_____

_____

_____

Since God owns it all, *every* money decision is a spiritual decision. Here's an example of how this mindset works out in a believer's life: When John Wesley, the founder of the Methodist Church, was told that his home had been destroyed by fire, he responded: "The Lord's house burned. One less responsibility for me!"

The Bible Says Money Is . . .	Our Reaction . . .
A blessing from God (Proverbs 10:22).	Be thankful!
A stewardship (Psalm 24:1; Romans 14:12).	Be responsible!
A test (Luke 12:48; 16:9-12).	Be faithful!
An indicator (Matthew 6:21).	Be aware of what you truly value.
A false hope (Proverbs 11:4; 1 Timothy 6:17).	Be wise!
A danger (Matthew 6:24; 13:22; 19:23; 1 Timothy 6:9-10).	Be wary!
A tool for honoring God and blessing others (Proverbs 3:9; Matthew 6:20).	Be generous!
A testimony (Ephesians 5:3).	Be sacrificial.

#2: Remember that giving is transformative.

What motivated this poor widow? She could have come up with a hundred reasons not to give. And so could we. So why did she do it? Why should we give?

7. What would you say are the best reasons to share the financial resources God has blessed you with?

_____

_____

_____

_____

Giving changes lives—including our own. Our generosity furthers the work of God. Just as importantly, practicing generosity changes us. It fosters trust that God will re-supply the money that we give away. Giving also combats our tendency to look to money for security, peace of mind, and happiness.

8. Read the following passage:

"But people who long to be rich fall into temptation and are trapped by many foolish and harmful desires that plunge them into ruin and destruction. For the love of money is the root of all kinds of evil. And some people, craving money, have wandered from the true faith and pierced themselves with many sorrows" (1 Timothy 6:9–10, NLT).

a. Record your thoughts on the lines below:

_____

_____

_____

_____

b. What are the spiritual benefits of giving money to the Lord?

_____

_____

_____

_____

#3: **Regard giving as the safest and wisest investment of all.**

We look at the annual *Forbes* List of "The 500 Richest People in the World" and are tempted to think: "These guys and gals have got it made. They're set! They're secure. If only I had money like that . . . "

> Generosity has nothing to do with your income and everything to do with your character.

Here's the truth: Even though our financial lingo includes terms like *securities*, *safety net*, *guaranteed returns*, and *futures*, Jesus tells us of the tremendous fragility of worldly wealth (Matthew 6:19–24). The markets are volatile. Scammers are everywhere. To put our hope in worldly riches is not only wrong, it's foolish.

Wise Warnings About Wealth

- "Prosperity knits a man to the world. He feels that he is 'finding his place in it,' when really it is finding its place in him." —C. S. Lewis

- "Money never stays with me. It would burn me if it did. I throw it out of my hands as soon as possible, lest it should find its way into my heart."—John Wesley

- "The fellow that has no money is poor. The fellow that has nothing but money is poorer still."—Billy Sunday

- "I am obliged to tell you that God does not need anything you have. He does not need a dime of your money. It is your own spiritual welfare at stake in such matters as these. . . . You have the right to keep what you have all to yourself—but it will rust and decay, and ultimately ruin you." —A. W. Tozer

James chided the rich, "You have hoarded wealth in the last days" (James 5:3). William Barclay translated this sentence, "You have piled up wealth in a world that is coming to an end."

Isn't that tragic? It's the classic bad investment, like putting all you've got in the stock market the day before it crashes! You amass a huge fortune, only to leave it all behind, or see it all disappear. What a waste!

Jesus made it clear that it's not wrong to accumulate wealth. In fact, it's good so long as it's the right kind of wealth stored up in the right place.

> "But store up for yourselves treasures *in heaven*, where moths and vermin do not destroy, and where thieves do not break in and steal" (Matthew 6:20).

Where should I give? To whom should I direct my support?

- Your family (1 Timothy 5:8)
- Your local church body to support collective ministry efforts and to support those who give themselves fully to God's work— missionaries, pastors, etc. (Acts 5:1-4)
- The poor (Proverbs 19:17)
- Christian brothers and sisters who are facing hard times (Galatians 6:10)
- Neighbors who are in trouble (Luke 10:30-37)
- Organizations and groups distinct from the church that are engaged in Christian ministry and advancing the kingdom of God
- Agencies devoted to relief work, helping the suffering

9. Someone once paraphrased Jesus' words this way: "You can't take it with you, but you *can* send it on ahead!" How do we "send our wealth on ahead to heaven"?

_____

_____

_____

_____

There is much, much more we could say about money and giving.[2] We've only scratched the surface of what the Bible teaches. To summarize, we've said that followers of Jesus practice sacrificial giving by consistently doing three things. They:

▷ Recognize "their" stuff is not really their stuff.

▷ Remember that giving is transformative.

▷ Regard giving as the safest and wisest investment of all.

---

2   *God and Money* by John Cortines and Gregory Baumer is an excellent resource for money planning. It outlines a simple framework and seven key principles for implementing radical generosity. *God and Money* is available at www.rose-publishing.com.

Take-Home Reflections

How the Average Person Spends Money[3]

After taxes, out of every dollar spent, families and/or individuals spend

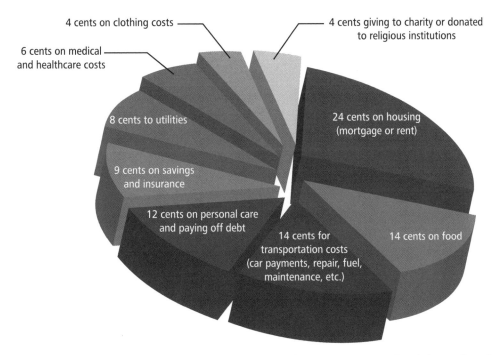

4 cents on clothing costs

4 cents giving to charity or donated to religious institutions

6 cents on medical and healthcare costs

8 cents to utilities

24 cents on housing (mortgage or rent)

9 cents on savings and insurance

12 cents on personal care and paying off debt

14 cents for transportation costs (car payments, repair, fuel, maintenance, etc.)

14 cents on food

"I do not believe one can settle how much we ought to give. I am afraid the only safe rule is to give more than we can spare. In other words, if our expenditure on comforts, luxuries, amusements, etc., is up to the standard common among those with the same income as our own, we are probably giving away too little. If our charities do not at all pinch or hamper us, I should say they are too small."—C. S. Lewis

Life Application

An important part of discipleship is learning how to apply God's truths to your life. Below are just a few ways you can start thinking about what you've learned and apply it to your daily life.

1. Memorize our verse, 2 Corinthians 9:6–7.

2. Look up the verses listed in "Ten Truths for Honoring God with Money." Prayerfully ask

---

3   U.S. Bureau of Labor Statistics, Consumer Expenditure Survey

God to show you an action step for each principle.

3. Wrestle with one or two of the following questions:

▷ What does it look like for you to "store up treasures in heaven"?

▷ God says to give to people who cannot repay us. Why do you think this is?

▷ God promises to meet our needs. Which promise speaks to you the most and why?

▷ God gives a lot of promises of reward to those who give. What is God saying to you?

▷ What are the dangers of putting our trust in money? If we trust in money rather than God, what happens?

▷ Is God inviting you to give to something? Make a list of possible people or organizations or types of organizations.

Ten Truths for Honoring God with Money

Biblical Principle	Passage	My Practical Action Step:
Determine to trust God, not money.	Revelation 3:17–21; Deuteronomy 8:18	
Am I trusting God, relying on my own wisdom, or trying to please someone else?	Proverbs 3:5–6, NLT; cf. 2 Corinthians 5:9–10	
Focus on the things that are most important.	Matthew 22:37–39; Proverbs 15:16–17	
Always remember God's enduring faithfulness.	Romans 8:32; Jeremiah 29:11	
Ask God to meet your financial needs.	Proverbs 30:8–9; Matthew 6:11	
Solicit divine wisdom in money matters.	James 1:5	
Act responsibly and with integrity in your handling of God's finances.	Romans 13:7	
Invest in eternal things.	Luke 12:33; Matthew 6:33	
Be generous and share what you have with others.	Deuteronomy 15:7; 2 Corinthians 9:6–7	
Cultivate contentment.	1 Timothy 6:7–8; Acts 20:33–35	
Praise God for his many generous blessings.	Psalm 112:1–5	

Laying Down Your Life for Others

> "Each of you should use whatever gift you have received to serve others, as faithful stewards of God's grace in its various forms."
> —1 Peter 4:10

The parents at Bayside Church approached their minister and church board with a request that the church hire a new youth pastor. "We're a young church that's filled with preadolescent kids," they reasoned, "We're located just two blocks from Bayside High. We should get someone to come in and work with our teens and shepherd them through the tough teen years."

The board agreed. After much prayer and a regional search lasting several months, Bayside hired Jason, a sharp, energetic guy with teens of his own to come and serve in this capacity.

Everything was great for three months. The new youth pastor spent time asking lots of questions, meeting families, getting to know kids, becoming familiar with the community. Then he called a parents' meeting. In that meeting, he presented an ambitious plan built around youth small groups. It's a plan that calls for a *lot* of adult volunteers.

The next day several parents called the church office. "We hired this guy to minister to our teens. But now he's asking *us* to sign up to work with them!" they complained. "Doesn't he understand the job description of a minister!?"

1. What do *you* think of when you hear the word "minister"? Write down any words, phrases, images, or thoughts that come to mind:

_____

_____

_____

_____

_____

> "One of the principal rules of religion is, to lose no occasion of serving God. And, since he is invisible to our eyes, we are to serve him in our neighbour; which he receives as if done to himself in person, standing visibly before us."
> —John Wesley

Check out the Apostle Paul's description of how Jesus designed his church to function. (Note: It's the passage that Jason uses to guide his own ministerial philosophy):

"He gave the apostles, the prophets, the evangelists, the shepherds and teachers, to equip the saints for the work of ministry, for building up the body of Christ" (Ephesians 4:11–12, ESV).[4]

2. According to these verses, what is the role of church leaders? What is the role of "the saints"—regular church members?

_____

_____

_____

_____

_____

_____

How about that? According to this passage, it isn't the professional clergy who are supposed to do all the hands-on working and serving and ministry. It's the saints—regular church members. The Apostle Paul describes a system in which pastors and teachers and other church leaders spend their time and efforts "equipping"—training and encouraging—the members of the congregation.

---

4   The NIV translates this last phrase "to equip his people for works of *service*." All through the New Testament those two words—ministry and service—are used interchangeably. To minister is to serve. To serve is to minister. All of God's people are to work at serving.

3. Read the following examples of churches.

  ▶ a church with five very gifted and talented staff members and a congregation that mostly sat back and watched the professional clergy use their gifts

  ▶ a church staff of three pastors committed to helping 100 willing and available volunteers discover and develop and use their gifts to minister to others

Explain which church would have the biggest impact and why.

_____

_____

_____

_____

_____

In this lesson we will see three things about ministry or service:

  ▶ Disciples are *called* to serve

  ▶ Disciples are *gifted* to serve

  ▶ Disciples must be *obedient* to serve.

Bible Study

Disciples Are Called to Serve

  ▶ "For even the Son of Man did not come to be served, but to serve, and to give his life as a ransom for many" (Mark 10:45).

  ▶ "In your relationships with one another, have the same mindset as Christ Jesus: Who, being in very nature God, did not consider equality with God something to be used to his own advantage; rather, he made himself nothing by taking the very nature of a servant" (Philippians 2:5–7).

  ▶ "You, my brothers and sisters, were called to be free. But do not use your freedom to indulge the flesh; rather, serve one another humbly in love" (Galatians 5:13).

It's clear that Jesus came to serve. It could be argued from Mark 10:45 that his entire life was one continuous act of service. It's also clear that those who follow Jesus are expected to act like Jesus.

4. What can make it difficult to follow Jesus and serve others?

_____

_____

_____

Disciples Are Gifted to Serve

In four different places—1 Corinthians 12, Romans 12, Ephesians 4, and 1 Peter 4, the Scripture speaks of something called *spiritual gifts*. A spiritual gift is best defined as a God-given ability for service to and through the body of Christ.

> "The Great Commission is the greatest command, given by the greatest Commander, to the greatest army, for the greatest task ever. . . . Unfortunately, some have forgotten that the God who assigned us this great task also assigned us the means to fulfill the task—people, men and women whom God has equipped to fulfill that task, men and women with God-given gifts— spiritual gifts." —Larry Gilbert

God sees to it that every believer has at least one gift (1 Corinthians 12:11, 18; 1 Peter 4:10). These supernatural abilities aren't given to call attention to the individuals who have them, but to glorify God and bless others. All these divine abilities are important for the healthy functioning of the body. The Greek word for these gifts is *charisma*—a form of *charis*, the word translated "grace." God distributes these gifts, or graces, as he sees fit, and never on the basis of merit (1 Corinthians 12:4–6, 11).

Most Common Christian Understanding of the Gifts:

▷ Some believers hold firmly that these four gifts were limited to a period between Jesus' ascension and the death of the last Apostle, Jesus' beloved disciple John (about AD 90). People who hold this view are known as *cessationists*.

▷ Other Christians affirm the continuation of all of the gifts. They are *continuationists*.

▷ Many other believers fall in an in-between category, "open but cautious."

▷ Still others believe that some of the four gifts continue, while others have ceased.

Whatever view we take, we must remember that according to Paul, the spiritual gifts are meant to promote the unity of the body (1 Corinthians 12:12; Ephesians 4:12–13). In the letters of Paul, the unity of the body is necessary for the church's growth. The alternative, disunity and spiritual arrogance, tears down the church.

5. Up until now, what has been your understanding of spiritual gifts?

_____

_____

_____

_____

Disciples Are Obedient to Serve

> "Trying to do the Lord's work in your own strength is the most confusing, exhausting, and tedious of all work. But when you are filled with the Holy Spirit, then the ministry of Jesus just flows out of you." —Corrie Ten Boom

Our verse for this lesson says: "Each of you should use whatever gift you have received to serve others, as faithful stewards of God's grace in its various forms" (1 Peter 4:10).

In Bible times a steward was the most trusted servant in a household. This individual was given authority over the master's estate and possessions. Anyone in the household with needs would ask the steward, who would then dispense whatever was needed.

The "Sweet Spot" of Service

Sometimes needs arise and we have to do things we may have zero desire to do or engage in tasks for which we are not exactly gifted. But when we get to address real *needs* that we have a *passion* to solve using our unique *gifts* and abilities, that's a very special blessing.

The apostle Peter tells us that the Lord has given each disciple a spiritual gift which others need (1 Corinthians 12:7). When we use our gift(s), we, in effect, dispense God's grace to others.

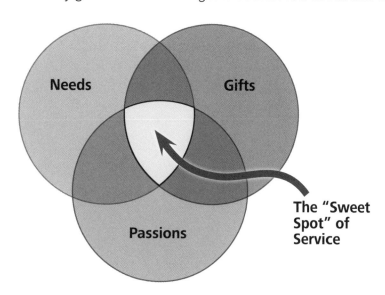

Needs / Gifts / Passions

The "Sweet Spot" of Service

Do you know what your spiritual gifts are? You can prayerfully discover your gifting in a variety of ways:

▶ *Examination* (via spiritual gift questionnaires—like the one on the following two pages)

▶ *Evaluation* (of your Christian history and experiences); *experimentation* with various new ministries

▶ *Enjoyment* (considering which acts of service have been most fulfilling to you)

▶ *Effectiveness* (considering where you have seen the most fruitfulness in ministry)

As with faith, prayer, and evangelism, it's not enough merely to study this topic. Being a follower of Jesus means rolling up your sleeves and diving in. We have to take action and get busy.

6. Now that you've studied a bit about this idea of being called and gifted to minister to others, what—specifically and practically—does service look like in your life today? What would you like it to look like in the days to come?

_____

_____

_____

_____

_____

_____

_____

_____

_____

_____

Take-Home Reflections

Good Reasons to Serve	Bad Reasons to Serve
Jesus served and we're called to be like him.	To avoid looking like a slacker
"Servant" is every disciple's new, true identity.	To alleviate guilt or pressure that others are laying on me
God has graced us with important abilities, skills, experiences, and blessings.	To show myself spiritually superior to those who don't serve
The world is a needy place. Jesus called us to serve the needy.	To put others in my debt
We are transformed as we engage in the process of serving others.	To try to win God's approval—and to avoid his displeasure for not serving
Serving is rewarding (both now and forever).	To compel others to serve me in return

Life Application

An important part of discipleship is learning how to apply God's truths to your life. Below are just a few ways you can start thinking about what you've learned and apply it to your daily life.

1. Memorize our memory verse, 1 Peter 4:10.

   "Each of you should use whatever gift you have received to serve others, as faithful stewards of God's grace in its various forms."

2. Read carefully and meditatively the story of Jesus washing his disciples' feet in John 13. On a separate sheet of paper journal any insights or "aha!" moments.

3. Complete the "Spiritual Gift Questionnaire" that follows.

Spiritual Gift Questionnaire

This questionnaire is one of many tools to help you discern where you fit in the church's many ministries. It can help you to either learn or confirm areas of affinity—areas that you naturally tend to focus on. But as with most spiritual gifts tests, it is not meant to definitively tell you what your gift is. Simply knowing your spiritual gifts is not the goal, but rather knowing how to serve God as a member of Christ's body is the real goal.

> Ask God for guidance and wisdom to find your place in the church's ministry.
> Your life experience can be a good guide to find your interest and abilities.
> Be mindful of the needs of your church. Sometimes, God will call you to minister—serve—in places you might not prefer. The calling may be temporary or long term.
> Be ready, willing, and courageous. Obedience is challenging.
> Listen to the encouragement, wisdom, and guidance of other members of the body of Christ.
> Be prayerful about finding God's will for you.

For each question, choose a response between 0 and 3 as follows:

3 Consistently, almost always true   **2** Most of the time, usually true   **1** Some of the time, once in a while   **0** Not at all, never

---

1. _____ I am able to communicate effectively the message of salvation through Christ Jesus.
2. _____ I make critical decisions when necessary.
3. _____ I rejoice when meeting needs through sharing my possessions.
4. _____ I enjoy studying.
5. _____ I thrive when trusting God in difficult situations.
6. _____ I actively meet physical and practical needs.
7. _____ I can analyze events or ideas from different points of view.
8. _____ I naturally encourage others.
9. _____ I am acutely in tune with the emotions of other people.
10. _____ I am a cheerful giver.
11. _____ Yielding to God's will gives me great joy.
12. _____ It is very important for me to do things for people in need.
13. _____ I can identify those who need encouragement.
14. _____ I am sensitive to the hurts of people.
15. _____ I am sensitive to new truths and to how they apply to specific situations.
16. _____ I have experience with organizing ideas, resources, time, and people effectively.
17. _____ I am able to discern when sermons or teachings do not conform to the Scriptures.
18. _____ I can trust in God even in very difficult moments.
19. _____ I can discern where God wants a group to go and help it get there.
20. _____ I have the ability and desire to teach.
21. _____ I am sensitive to what people need.
22. _____ I have experience making effective and efficient plans for accomplishing the goals of a group.
23. _____ I can explain Scripture in simple and accessible ways.
24. _____ I spend time digging into facts.
25. _____ Sharing Christ with nonbelievers comes naturally to me.
26. _____ I can discern the motivation of persons and movements.
27. _____ I can delegate and assign meaningful work.
28. _____ I detect when people experience stress and distress.
29. _____ I desire to give generously and unpretentiously to worthwhile projects and ministries.
30. _____ I can relate God's truths to specific situations.
31. _____ I can organize facts into meaningful relationships.
32. _____ I can detect honesty (and dishonesty) when people share their religious experiences.
33. _____ I look for ways to encourage and comfort others around me.
34. _____ I am able to help people flourish in their ministries.
35. _____ I can make complex ideas and doctrines simple and accessible to others.
36. _____ I look for opportunities to establish relationships with non-believers.

Write your answer for each question, then add your answers for each gift. Pay attention to 2's or 3's. These are likely the gifts you are currently leaning toward.

Gift	Question Number	Your Answer	Total
Discernment	17		
	26		
	32		
Exhortation	8		
	13		
	33		
Evangelism	1		
	25		
	36		
Faith	5		
	11		
	18		
Giving	3		
	10		
	29		
Guidance	16		
	22		
	27		
Help/Serving	6		
	12		
	21		
Knowledge	4		
	24		
	31		
Leadership	2		
	19		
	34		
Mercy	9		
	14		
	28		
Teaching	20		
	23		
	35		
Wisdom	7		
	15		
	30		

Topic 9: Evangelism

Sharing the Message of Your New Life in Christ

"But in your hearts revere Christ as Lord. Always
be prepared to give an answer to everyone who
asks you to give the reason for the hope that you
have. But do this with gentleness and respect."

—1 Peter 3:15

Evangelism simply means sharing the good news of God's love for the world through Christ. But in today's world, sometimes it comes across differently. What comes into your mind when you hear the word "evangelism"?

- ❏ A silver-tongued television preacher smiling at the camera and asking for money
- ❏ A sweating preacher who is flailing and yelling at his congregation
- ❏ A red-faced person who is arguing obnoxiously with a skeptic about the Bible
- ❏ Putting Christian bumper stickers on your car
- ❏ Turning off all your friends by being preachy and weird
- ❏ Other (write on blank line below):

_____

The sad but true fact is that many Christians, for many reasons, don't talk about their faith to non-believers.

Primary Reasons Christians Don't Share Their Faith[5]

Reason	Example
Fear	"I'm scared of what others might say; how people might react."
Lack of training	"No one ever showed me how to talk about spiritual matters. I wouldn't know what to say!"
Minimal contact with unbelievers	"I mostly spend time with my Christian friends."

---

5   "Successful Witnessing," *The Compass*, www.cru.org/content/dam/cru/legacy/2012/01/successfulwitnessing.pdf.

Reason	Example
Shaky theology	"God is in control; he knows who is going to become Christian, so I don't need to say anything. Besides, who am I to foist my views on others? People have to find their own way."
A lack of concern	"I've got a lot going on in my life; I really need to focus now on my schooling/career/etc."
Losing sight of the power of the gospel	"As if my pitiful words and life could make a difference!"
Disobedience	"Bottom line: I just don't want to do that."
Forgetting what successful evangelism is	"I have talked to twelve people about Jesus, and none have become Christians. So obviously I'm not called to evangelize."

And yet, a careful reading of the gospels shows that a disciple is a person who follows Jesus—to *know* Jesus and his teaching; to *grow* more like Jesus; and to *go* for Jesus, serving others and making new disciples. In this lesson we're looking hard at that third aspect of discipleship: going out into the world with Jesus. And specifically, talking about the gospel—doing evangelism, witnessing, sharing your faith, etc.

Bible Study

1. Have you ever tried to have a spiritual conversation with someone who was not a follower of Jesus, and if so, what happened?

_____

_____

_____

_____

2. If you are reluctant to talk to others about spiritual matters, what are *your* reasons?

_____

_____

_____

_____

_____

The apostle Peter wrote his first epistle to believers who were being persecuted for their Christian beliefs. If ever there were a group of folks tempted to be "close-mouthed" about Jesus, this would have been the group. And yet, in 1 Peter 3:13–18, we find a challenge for them to verbalize their faith:

> "Who is going to harm you if you are eager to do good? But even if you should suffer for what is right, you are blessed. 'Do not fear their threats; do not be frightened.' But in your hearts revere Christ as Lord. Always be prepared to give an answer to everyone who asks you to give the reason for the hope that you have. But do this with gentleness and respect, keeping a clear conscience, so that those who speak maliciously against your good behavior in Christ may be ashamed of their slander. For it is better, if it is God's will, to suffer for doing good than for doing evil. For Christ also suffered once for sins, the righteous for the unrighteous, to bring you to God. He was put to death in the body but made alive in the Spirit."

3. Before we look at it more deeply, what jumps out to you from this passage?

_____

_____

_____

_____

_____

Evangelism Myths and Truths

Based on the passage above, work your way through the following chart, reflecting on the wrong notions many believers have about evangelism and how this passage refutes these evangelism myths.

Evangelism MYTH	Seeing the good news as GOOD NEWS!	Evangelism TRUTH
Sharing your faith depends on having a slick, prepared speech.	"in your hearts revere Christ as Lord . . ."	Sharing your faith depends on a surrendered heart.
You have to know a ton of theology.		You have to know Christ as Lord.

Evangelism MYTH	Seeing the good news as GOOD NEWS!	Evangelism TRUTH
It's the pastor's job.		It's the job description of every disciple.
Witnessing is an activity.	**"Always be prepared to give an answer . . ."**	Witnessing is a way of life.
I prefer to let my life do the talking.		We need to add words to our good deeds and humble, loving attitudes.
Nobody is interested in the gospel.	**"to everyone who asks you to give the reason for the hope that you have . . ."**	People are interested in a life that's being transformed by the gospel.
Christians spread the gospel best by inviting Christians to religious gatherings.		Disciples spread the gospel most effectively by breaking out of their church groups and permeating the rest of the world.
Evangelism means confronting people—usually strangers—in a hard-hitting, and usually awkward, offensive, and abrasive way.	**"But do this with gentleness and respect . . ."**	Evangelism means loving the people God has placed in your life until they ask you why. And then, with great sensitivity, gently introducing them to Jesus.
A witness should "have it all together."	**"keeping a clear conscience . . ."**	A witness should be authentic and real, sharing his or her own struggles.
We should use whatever means are necessary to get the message out.		We should always be honest and ethical in our interactions with unbelievers, treating them with the same respect we want to receive.
Success in sharing your faith means that a non-Christian prays "the sinner's prayer."	**"so that those who speak maliciously against your good behavior in Christ may be ashamed of their slander."**	Success in sharing your faith means that God works in hearts in his way and his time, using our witness as he sees fit.

4. As you look at that chart, would you say your understanding of evangelism has been based more on myth or on truth? Why?

_____

_____

_____

One of the best and easiest ways to share the gospel with others is to simply tell the story of your spiritual journey. The Bible word for this holy habit is "witness." What's a witness? It's someone who has experienced something and who gives testimony about that experience to others (1 John 1:3). A witness has seen something with his own eyes. She's heard something with her own ears. A witness is nothing more than a truth-teller.

"It is not our work to make men believe: that is the work of the Holy Spirit."—D. L. Moody

You don't have to be a theologian or pastor to learn to tell others about your own experience with Christ. Your testimony is just a succinct telling of how you met Jesus and how He has altered and continues to transform your life. It means sharing the ups and downs of your journey of faith.

Sharing your spiritual story is a valuable skill. It's an effective tool for several reasons:

▶ Who can argue with a changed, authentic life? People can debate the Bible or quibble over theology, but no one can deny that something significant has happened to you.

▶ Your personal testimony can be adapted to all sorts of unique situations.

▶ God often uses the story of a person's spiritual journey to pave the way for deeper discussions of the gospel.

So how to do it? How can you become adept at "sharing your testimony"? Here are some basics to get you started.

5. First, take a few minutes to read Acts 26:1–31, the apostle Paul's testimony to King Agrippa about his own encounter with Jesus. What stands out to you about Paul's witness here?

Do you notice how Paul spoke simply, logically, and chronologically? He began by speaking about his life *before* he met Christ on the Damascus Road (vss. 4–11). Then he related the circumstances surrounding his actual encounter with Jesus (vss. 12–20). Finally, he shared how his life changed *after* believing in Christ (verses 21–23).

That's an easy and clear outline to follow in preparing our own testimonies. Let's do it!

Writing Your Testimony

6. Answer the following questions lettered *a* through *f*. Then, take these answers and copy them to a separate sheet of paper or type them into your computer. Make whatever adjustments are needed for clarity and flow. The end result will be a concise and clear rendering of your personal testimony.

On the lines below, jot some notes and recollections about your own life prior to placing your faith in Christ. Perhaps you struggled with one or more of the following. And by the way, it's okay if these struggles continue to affect you. It's your *growth, trust, and persistence*—thanks to the strengthening of Christ—that matter.

- ❏ Feeling far from God
- ❏ Gnawing inner emptiness
- ❏ Lack of peace
- ❏ Fear of death
- ❏ Family dysfunction
- ❏ Longing for meaning in life
- ❏ Traumatic childhood hurts
- ❏ Feelings of insignificance

- ❏ Loneliness
- ❏ Feeling unloved
- ❏ Insecurity
- ❏ Immense guilt
- ❏ Desire for control
- ❏ Addictive behaviors
- ❏ Lack of purpose
- ❏ Emotional instability

a. Describe yourself before you met Christ in a personal way.

_____

_____

_____

_____

_____

_____

Oftentimes people try without success to solve their own problems. Perhaps this is your story as well. Maybe you looked for answers to the deep needs of your heart through a job, money, fun experiences, or popularity—even being religious? Maybe you thought academic success or athletic achievement or romance would "save" you.

b. Describe some of *your* failed attempts to fix your own problems.

_____

_____

_____

_____

_____

Now, recall the circumstances surrounding how you were drawn to Christ. What made you consider him as the solution to your deepest needs?

c. Identify the specific events that led to your trusting in Jesus. If this was a long-term process, summarize it, but don't leave out important details.

_____

_____

_____

_____

_____

d. State clearly the steps you took to put your faith in Christ. If God drew you to himself through a particular Bible verse, share that verse.

_____

_____

_____

_____

_____

However you describe this life-changing moment, make sure to make the gospel clear. This includes the following truths:

▶ "I realized I was a sinner, separated from God."

▶ "I saw that the penalty for sin is death."

▶ "I understood that Jesus paid the penalty for my sins."

▶ "I put my trust in Christ alone and what He did for me."

Now very concisely, talk about your life *since* coming into a relationship with Jesus. Your goal here is to show the difference that Christ is making in your life. You don't need to show one-hundred percent victory over every difficulty. Simply sharing your confidence—through examples—that the Lord is walking beside you through the problems, will help your listener understand.

e. What are the biggest changes that have happened in your life?

_____

_____

_____

_____

_____

Be sure to conclude with a statement along the lines of, "And, of course, in addition to the amazing benefit of being accepted in this life, I also have the promise of heaven." A statement like this often leads to a deeper conversation of spiritual matters. Your friend may ask, "How can you say that? How can *anyone* say that? How can you know *for sure*?"

f. Write your closing statement.

_____

_____

_____

_____

_____

_____

"I look upon this world as a wrecked vessel. God has given me a lifeboat and said, 'Moody, save all you can.'"—D. L. Moody

Take-Home Reflections

Top Ten Testimony Tips!

▶ No two testimonies are alike because no two lives are. Don't try to copy someone else's story. God can and will use your own unique experience to speak to others. Be real. Be authentic. There's an old Yiddish proverb that says, "If you try to be someone else, who will be you?"

▶ If you met Christ as an adult, you may have a distinct *before, how,* and *after.* If you trusted Christ as a child, you may not be able to report radical changes in behavior; nevertheless, you ought to be able to point to some concrete ways Christ is changing you now or has changed you in the past (in attitudes, goals, challenges, desires, etc.).

▶ Avoid Christian clichés. Many Biblical words and phrases that are meaningful to believers (saved, sin, lost, born again, live in your heart, washed in the blood, sanctified, etc.) are meaningless to unbelievers. Translate Christian jargon into normal English.

▶ Avoid controversial statements or subjects. For example, going off on a rant against alcohol may turn off a skeptical person.

▶ Don't criticize specific churches, individuals, or groups.

▶ There is no need to share a lot of the seamy details of your life before meeting Christ. Be discreet.

▶ Keep your testimony warm and personal. Don't get preachy and wordy. Make it a point to say "I" and "me" rather than "you." This is your story, and yours alone. God deals differently with each person.

▶ Practice sharing your testimony with a spouse, child, parent, Christian friend, or small group until it becomes second nature. Then ask God for opportunities to share your testimony with non-Christian friends and acquaintances.

▶ Don't bore people with tons of unnecessary details. A succinct summary—three to four minutes at absolute most—is sufficient. You want to arouse curiosity. You want, when you're done, people asking for *more* details rather than thinking, "I thought he or she would *never* shut up!"

▶ If you can, include a meaningful Bible verse. God's Word is far more powerful than anything we might say. It has the power to change hearts and lives (2 Timothy 3:16–17). If you quote a verse, make sure it's one that speaks about the hope that Christ brings or about the free gift of the gospel (John 10:10, Ephesians 2:8–9). It's usually a good idea to do this from one of the more modern, easy-to-understand translations like the *New Living Translation* (NLT), the *New International Version* (NIV), or the *English Standard Version* (ESV).

Life Application

An important part of discipleship is learning how to apply God's truths to your life. Below are just a few ways you can start thinking about what you've learned and apply it to your daily life.

1. Memorize our memory verse, 1 Peter 3:15:

   "But in your hearts revere Christ as Lord. Always be prepared to give an answer to everyone who asks you to give the reason for the hope that you have. But do this with gentleness and respect."

2. Read through the suggestions in "How to Create Opportunities to Talk About Your Faith," on the next page. These suggestions help you weave your testimony into everyday conversations.

3. Wrestle with one or two of the questions in the right-hand column.

   ▷ How can a rich, authentic relationship with Jesus—and submission to his Lordship (1 Peter 3:15)—make a difference in how we share our faith?

   ▷ Which is more important: "walking the walk"— Christian living—or "talking the talk"—telling others about Christ? Which are you better at and why?

   ▷ Why is it that some Christians have no meaningful contacts with unbelievers?

   ▷ Why would Christians get defensive when skeptics attack our faith?

   ▷ Does Peter's command to respond "with gentleness and respect" mean that we can never say "hard" things to non-Christian friends?

   ▷ Make a list of five people with whom you'd like to discuss spiritual matters. Pray for them. We should always talk to God about people before we talk to people about God.

How to Create Opportunities to Talk About Your Faith

▷ Don't spend all your time with church people! Build relationships with those who don't know Christ! Move toward them in love. Love them because God does. Love them with no strings attached. Win the right to be heard.

▷ Don't condemn unbelievers for living like unbelievers. That's what they are! Their biggest need isn't a lifestyle change—it's Jesus! Accept them as they are. Many of them are leery about judgmental Christians. It's the Holy Spirit's job to convict them of sin and repentance, not yours.

▷ Open your life. Talk about everyday stuff (family, hobbies, job, school, friends, children, relationships, etc.). Listen attentively for expressed needs such as family problems or stress in school or at work. For example, if your friend says, "I'm really worried about my son . . . " maybe you can sympathize and tactfully share how Christ has helped you in a similar situation—or how he brought you through your own difficult teen years.

▷ Discuss personal struggles and needs—both past and present. "Did I ever tell you how I survived my divorce?" "We're going through a rough patch financially, and it's nerve-wracking, but you know what? Never in my life have I felt abandoned by God. He has always provided for us."

▷ After sharing something Christ has done or is doing in your life, ask a question like "Have you ever experienced anything like that?" or "Does that make sense?"

▷ Don't argue. Absolutely refuse to debate. No one ever got dragged kicking and screaming into the kingdom of God! Today may not be God's timing.

▷ Never "dump the truck." Better to say less, and have them ask for more, than to say too much and have them looking for the nearest exit.

▷ Piggyback off contemporary situations and news stories. Ask thought-provoking questions. For example, when a friend brings up how so many politicians seem to tap into and prey upon voters' fears: "Why do think people are so afraid? What are the things that scare you? What do you do when you feel fearful?" After listening thoughtfully, maybe you can say something like, "You know, I can certainly relate. The world is a pretty scary place. But that's something my faith has helped me with . . . "

▷ If it's clear your friend is uncomfortable, end on a positive note. Communicate love and acceptance. Allow the Holy Spirit to set the pace. He opens and closes doors of opportunity.

Embracing God's Heart for the World

> "But you will receive power when the Holy Spirit comes on you; and you will be my witnesses in Jerusalem, and in all Judea and Samaria, and to the ends of the earth."
>
> —Acts 1:8

In 1916, a young Irish woman by the name of Irene Webster-Smith went to Japan with the Japan Evangelistic Band (JEB) and began to minister to prostitutes. Eventually, she decided that it would be better to prevent girls from becoming prostitutes in the first place—or in her words, "Erect a fence at the top of the precipice rather than driving an ambulance at the bottom." To that end she began to adopt unwanted babies and began the Sunrise Home. Her work continued until 1940, when she was forced to leave Japan at the advent of World War II.

Following the war, when General Douglas MacArthur was supervising the rebuiliding of Japan, he personally invited Irene to come back and minister to war criminals who were to be executed. Irene was able to lead fourteen of these war criminals and some of their guards to Christ.

In her last years, Irene, who was known as *Sensei*, worked with InterVarsity Fellowship, teaching Japanese college students about Christ and founding the Ochanomizu Christian Student Center at Tokyo University.

1. When someone brings up the topic of *missions* what sorts of thoughts and ideas run through your mind?

_____

_____

_____

_____

Perhaps you've heard of the Great Commission of Christ. This biblical passage is what gets Christians and churches thinking about the global task of making disciples.

The Great Commission

"God has made you for global purposes. God has made you for something very large."—John Piper

"All authority in heaven and on earth has been given to me. Therefore go and make disciples of all nations, baptizing them in the name of the Father and of the Son and of the Holy Spirit, and teaching them to obey everything I have commanded you. And surely I am with you always, to the very end of the age" (Matthew 28:18–20).

2. Do you think Christ's command to "make disciples of all nations" means we all need to pack up our belongings and move to foreign soil? Why or why not?

_____

_____

_____

Some believers regard cross-cultural ministry as "one more thing the church does"—an optional program, sort of like the men's softball team or the hand bell choir. Others cringe from guilt at the "m" word, because they're not involved. Still others feel they have no way to contribute to God's global cause.

In this session, we hope to demonstrate, first, that making disciples of all nations isn't a side venture of the church, it's our reason for being! Second, we want to explore some very practical ways ordinary followers of Jesus can have a worldwide impact, often without leaving their own zip code!

Let's begin!

Bible Study

God has a heart for the nations of the world.

The New Testament Greek word commonly translated "nation" is *ethnos* (Matthew 28:19). This is the word from which we get our English word "ethnic." That's the idea—a distinct ethnic group, people, or race.

> In North America, there are more than 1,430 distinct people groups and almost 147 of these are considered "unreached."

We tend to think of nations as political entities or geographical areas marked by lines on a map. But God in his Word always focuses on groups that share a common affinity and self-identity—cultural background and language. Think of the Kurdish People, spread out across Turkey, Syria, Iraq and Iran; the Choctaw Nation in the United States; or the Maasai Tribe who spill out of southern Kenya into northern Tanzania.

> An unreached people group refers to an ethnic group that lacks an indigenous, self-propagating Christian church movement.

After God created the world (Genesis 1–2) and mankind sinned (Genesis 3–9), we see the rise of nations. These distinct peoples—with divine help—begin to spread out across the earth (Genesis 10–11).

Then, in Genesis 12, we see God choose one man and give him remarkable promises:

"The LORD had said to Abram, 'Go from your country, your people and your father's household to the land I will show you. I will make you into a great nation, and I will bless you; I will make your name great, and you will be a blessing. I will bless those who bless you, and whoever curses you I will curse; and all peoples on earth will be blessed through you'" (Genesis 12:1–3).

3. What reason does God give for blessing Abram (later called Abraham)?

_____

_____

_____

_____

_____

Clearly, since humanity's "fall" into sin (Genesis 3), God's desire has been to rescue and bless all peoples. God has a heart for the nations of the world! Carefully read and consider the following passages from Genesis to Revelation:

▶ "I will make your descendants as numerous as the stars in the sky and will give them all these lands, and through your offspring all nations on earth will be blessed" (Genesis 26:4).

▶ "May your ways be known throughout the earth, your saving power among people everywhere. May the nations praise you, O God. Yes, may all the nations praise you" (Psalm 67:2–3, NLT).

▶ "God blesses us, that all the ends of the earth may fear Him" (Psalm 67:7, NASB).

▶ "All the nations you have made will come and worship before you, Lord; they will bring glory to your name" (Psalm 86:9).

▶ "Praise the LORD, all nations; laud Him, all peoples!" (Psalm 117:1, NASB).

▶ "This gospel of the kingdom will be preached in the whole world as a testimony to all nations, and then the end will come" (Matthew 24:14).

▶ "He said to me, 'Go, for I will send you far away to the Gentiles'" (Acts 22:21, ESV).

▶ "Is it not written: 'My house will be called a house of prayer for all nations'? But you have made it 'a den of robbers'" (Mark 11:17).

▶ "Moved by the Spirit, he went into the temple courts. When the parents brought in the child Jesus to do for him what the custom of the Law required, Simeon took him in his arms and praised God, saying: 'Sovereign Lord, as you have promised, you may now dismiss your servant in peace. For my eyes have seen your salvation, which you have prepared in the sight of all nations: a light for revelation to the Gentiles, and the glory of your people Israel'" (Luke 2:27–32).

▶ "After this I looked, and there before me was a great multitude that no one could count, from every nation, tribe, people and language, standing before the throne and before the Lamb. They were wearing white robes and were holding palm branches in their hands. And they cried out in a loud voice: 'Salvation belongs to our God, who sits on the throne, and to the Lamb'" (Revelation 7:9–10).

4. What do you see here in all this talk about nations, peoples, and Gentiles?

---

5. According to the passage above from Revelation 7, where is history headed?

_____

_____

6. How would you summarize God's desire, his heart, for the peoples of the world?

_____

_____

Cultivating a Missionary Heart like God's

God doesn't call every believer to move to a foreign country. But he does want us to think about the world, pray for its needs, and do our part in fulfilling the Great Commission—even if it's a behind-the-scenes role. There's an old saying that some can go, most can give, and all can pray. The more we learn and engage, the more we'll sense our heart beating for the nations.

Here are thirty-one simple, doable, and creative ways to be a "World Christian" right where you are now.

▶ Read the book of Acts in one sitting. Imagine traveling with Peter or Paul, doing evangelism, discipling believers, planting new churches.

▶ Discover a wealth of information about reaching the unreached people groups of the world at www.joshuaproject.net.

▶ Offer to serve on your church's missions committee, or on a long- or short-term missions team.

▶ Get a whirlwind short-course in the history of world missions by reading Ruth Tucker's missions classic From Jerusalem to Irian Jaya.

▶ Get a list of church-sponsored missionaries. Memorize their names and where they serve. Find out their birthdays, anniversaries, etc. and fuss over them on those special days.

▶ Take the life-changing Perspectives on the World Christian Movement course. To find out about classes in your area check out www.perspectives.org.

▶ Get your passport or make sure it is up to date just in case you have the opportunity to go on a short-term mission trip.

▶ Every chance you get, invite furloughed or retired missionaries into your home for dinner. Let family members and roommates rub shoulders with disciples whose hearts beat for the nations.

▶ If you're an empty nester, single, or a family with an extra bedroom in your home, inquire about missionary couples or families on furlough. Offer to host them whenever they pass through your area.

▶ Identify culturally diverse people who live in your neighborhood. Reach out to them by inviting them over for dinner, asking them to go on a picnic, etc. In short, pray that God will enable you to develop a redemptive relationship with your neighbors.

▶ Begin asking the Lord of the harvest to send out workers into his harvest (Luke 10:2). Pray that some, even from your own church, would be thrust out into places of effective ministry among the unreached.

▶ Fast one day a week. Use those meal times to pray for an unreached people group. Give the money that you would have spent on groceries that day to a missionary working to plant a church among an unreached people group. If you estimate two dollars for breakfast, three dollars for lunch, and five dollars for supper, that would be ten dollars a week or forty dollars a month that could be spent supporting missions.

▶ If you are financially able, don't sell or trade in your old car. Instead, donate it to your favorite mission agency for use by missionaries who are home on furlough and must make frequent trips to visit their supporters.

▶ Email a missionary you know and love. Ask, "If I could buy you any two books to help you in what you're doing, what two titles would you want?" Order those desired resources and mail them to the missionary.

▶ Put an acrylic photo holder in the center of your dining table. Put a different missionary picture or prayer letter in it each day. Make these servants of God, their activities, and needs a regular part of your family's daily dining experience.

▶ Take a picture of your Sunday school class, family, or small group holding up a poster that says, "We love you and are lifting you up!" Mail it to a sponsored missionary family.

▶ If you have an area in your city where different ethnic groups live (Chinatown, little Havana, a Hispanic neighborhood, etc.), gather a friend or two and go on a prayer walk through that neighborhood. A "prayer walk" is just what it sounds like. You walk and pray at the same time—for the salvation of those in the area who don't know Christ, for workers to reach out to them, for believers in the area to be strong witnesses, etc.

▶ Get an international cookbook from the library and one night a week, try cooking a dish that would commonly be served and eaten in another country. Allow your whole family to experience life from a different perspective. For extra fun, check out a "travel videologue" about that country from your public library. These DVDs, usually 60 minutes in length, can give you a whirlwind, "up close and personal" peek at places and peoples around the globe!

▶ Make an appointment with a financial advisor about getting out of debt and living by a budget. For some, this is a long, slow, difficult process. For others, it requires only a minor adjustment in lifestyle. For all, it opens up new opportunities to live for the kingdom and to allocate more resources to eternal ventures.

▷ Start reading up on "International News." Many believers ignore these stories because they claim they don't understand political developments taking place around the world. The irony is that we will *never* come to understand global events until we make the effort to get informed.

▷ Visit an ethnic market in your community. Take your children and allow them to experience the different sights, sounds, and smells. Better yet, once every three months or so, visit an ethnic restaurant in your city.

▷ Have a garage sale and donate the proceeds to a missionary family in need. They get necessary funding. You get a de-cluttered attic, garage, basement, and closets!

▷ Get a copy of *Operation World*, the definitive prayer guide to every nation. This resource looks at the world country by country, gives a brief glimpse of what God is doing in each place, and suggests ways believers can pray. Find out more or get other resources at www.operationworld.org.

▷ Look at the labels on your clothing. If your shirt says "Made in Malaysia," pray for that country—for God to open eyes and hearts there, for the church there to grow and be strengthened and emboldened, for missionaries working there, etc.

▷ Surprise a missionary family with a care package filled with goodies and hard-to-find items. Make sure you first find out about customs requirements and restrictions—you don't want your gesture of love to cost your overseas friends an arm and a leg!

▷ Minister to a missionary family on furlough. Take them to lunch. Bring them a batch of cookies. Offer to provide childcare for an evening. Take him golfing or fishing. Take her shopping. Give the family a gift certificate.

▷ Almost all universities have sizable international student communities. These bright and influential visitors are often very open to your friendship. Many times the wives and children of such graduate and doctoral students lead lives of isolation and loneliness. If you live near a university, contact the International Student office and find out how you can reach out to these future leaders.

▷ Invite international students into your home and your life. Help them with English. Inform them about local customs. Have them teach you a song or authentic dance from their homeland. Or have them plan a native meal of two or three dishes. You buy the necessary ingredients; they come over and cook and tell you about their lives and culture.

▷ Consider offering your professional services (dental, medical, legal, accounting, etc.) for free to missionaries on furlough.

▷ Buy a small globe and make it a dining table centerpiece. At supper each night, discuss a different country. Learn the capital cities of the world.

The point is, whether you're a young professional, a small business owner, or a stay-at-home mom, you *can* play a role in God's global and eternal cause—right where you are. Every disciple can be a World Christian. Little acts of faithfulness can and do make an eternal difference.

7. What are some things you'd like to explore in terms of becoming a more missions-minded "world Christian"?

_____

_____

Take-Home Reflections

World Missions: By the Numbers (as of 2016)

7,300,000,000	People in the world
865,000,000	Muslims with no gospel witness
550,000,000	Unreached Hindus
275,000,000	Buddhists who haven't heard of Christ
4,190,000	Full-time Christian workers
16,761	Distinct people groups
6,500	Languages in the world
900	Number of churches for every unreached people group in the world
105	People who die every minute
1	Life you have to give

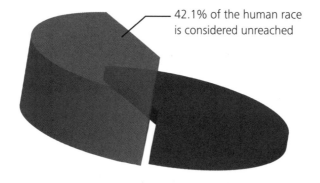

42.1% of the human race is considered unreached

Life Application

An important part of discipleship is learning how to apply God's truths to your life. Below are just a few ways you can start thinking about what you've learned and apply it to your daily life.

1. Memorize our memory verse, Acts 1:8.

    "But you will receive power when the Holy Spirit comes on you; and you will be my witnesses in Jerusalem, and in all Judea and Samaria, and to the ends of the earth."

2. Learn about the 10/40 Window:

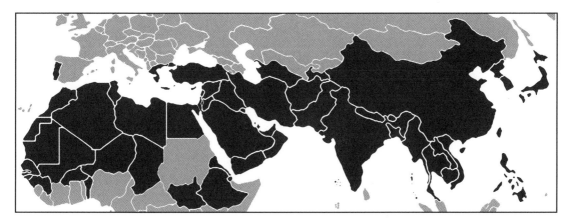

    Within the rectangle formed between ten degrees north and forty degrees north latitude lies much of Asia, the Middle East, and North Africa.

    This land area is home to almost 5,500 unreached people groups and some three billion individuals. This is where most of the world's Muslims, Hindus, and Buddhists live. Many have never heard of Christ's love and sacrifice for them.

3. Ponder these words:

    "Most men are not satisfied with the permanent output of their lives. Nothing can wholly satisfy the life of Christ within his followers except the adoption of Christ's purpose toward the world he came to redeem. Fame, pleasure, and riches are but husks and ashes in contrast with the boundless and abiding joy of working with God for the fulfillment of his eternal plans. The men who are putting everything into Christ's undertaking are getting out of life its sweetest and most priceless rewards."
    —J. Campbell White

    Journal your thoughts on a separate sheet of paper.

4. Pray, asking the Lord, "What is my specific role in fulfilling the Great Commission?"

Leader Guide

Congratulations! You've either decided to lead a discipleship group, or you're thinking hard about it. Guess what? God does big things through small groups. When his people gather together, open his Word, and invite his Spirit to work, their lives are changed!

Do you feel intimidated yet?

Be comforted by this: even the great apostle Paul felt "in over his head" at times. When he went to Corinth to help people grasp God's truth, he admitted he was overwhelmed: "I came to you in weakness with great fear and trembling" (1 Corinthians 2:3). Later he wondered, "Who is equal to such a task?" (2 Corinthians 2:16).

Feelings of inadequacy are normal; every leader has them. What's more, they're actually healthy. They keep us dependent on the Lord. It is in our times of greatest weakness that God works most powerfully. The Lord assured Paul, "My grace is sufficient for you, for my power is made perfect in weakness" (2 Corinthians 12:9).

What is the goal of a discipleship group? Listen to what Jesus said to the disciples in the verses known as the Great Commission:

"Then Jesus came to them and said, 'All authority in heaven and on earth has been given to me. Therefore go and make disciples of all nations, baptizing them in the name of the Father and of the Son and of the Holy Spirit, and teaching them to obey everything I have commanded you. And surely I am with you always, to the very end of the age'" (Matthew 28:18–20).

Discipleship is about learning to follow God and then helping others do the same. God's ultimate goal for us is that we would become like Jesus Christ. This means that this study is not about filling our heads with more information. Rather, it is about undergoing transformation. We study and apply God's truth so that it will reshape our hearts and minds, and so that over time, we will become more and more like Jesus. And the best part is, he promises to be with us throughout the whole process, giving us the strength we need as we learn to walk in his footsteps alongside our fellow believers.

How To Use This Book

This workbook is part of a three-book study of discipleship by Rose Publishing: *Rose Discipleship Series*.

   ▶   Knowing: Basics of the Faith

   ▶   Growing: Fruits of the Spirit

   ▶   Going: Spiritual Practices

Each book contains ten topics and can be completed in ten weeks. The books can be completed in any order—it all depends on the unique needs of your church or discipleship group.

Each session in these studies has an introduction to the session topic, followed by three sections: Bible Study, Take-Home Reflections, and Life Application. The *Introduction* familiarizes your discipleship group to the topic. The *Bible Study* section examines how that topic is related to the Christian faith. In *Take-Home Reflections*, you'll find prompts to help participants meditate on the topic during the week. Finally, the *Life Application* offers a memory verse and reading material to help group members incorporate the topic into the rhythm of everyday life.

Below are some suggestions for how to structure your discipleship group's meeting time.

	30-Minute Session	**60-Minute Session**
Introduction	Open in prayer and introduce your group to the topic for the week. Read the topic Bible verse. *5 minutes*	Open in prayer and introduce your group to the topic for the week. Discuss the topic together. *15 minutes*
Bible Study	Read this section together. Members voluntarily share their answers to the questions. *20 minutes*	Read this section together. Members voluntarily share their answers to the questions. *20 minutes*
Take-Home Reflections	Group members may go through this section on their own during the week.	Group members may go through this section on their own during the week.
Life Application	Group members may go through this section on their own during the week.	Read the memory verse. Choose one or two questions for group members to voluntarily discuss. *15 minutes*
Prayer & Closing	Conclude with a brief prayer. *5 minutes*	Ask members to share prayer requests. Conclude with prayer. *10 minutes*

Here are some important truths to keep in mind as you embark on leading a discipleship group:

▶ God is the primary agent of transformation in a person's life. You can't rescue or "fix" anyone. See yourself, instead, as a human instrument in God's hands. The Holy Spirit alone knows what is best for each person. Trust him to work his will (not yours) in his own timing.

▶ Your job description is to be pure, available, and yielded to God. You are to be a conduit of God's love, grace, and truth. Your role is to ask God to work in your group members' lives—to believe that he sees and knows the deep needs of their hearts, to trust that he is at work, even when you can't see it.

▶ Though you can't save anyone or *make* anyone grow in the faith, you can:

✦ Pray
✦ Observe
✦ Come alongside
✦ Engage
✦ Accept
✦ Invite
✦ Ask good questions
✦ Listen
✦ Model
✦ Love
✦ Serve

✦ Share the gospel
✦ Open your heart and life
✦ Pass on your experiences
✦ Invest time
✦ Teach skills
✦ Remind
✦ Encourage
✦ Challenge
✦ Gently confront
✦ Be gracious and merciful

In short, you can do a *lot!*

▶ Those who happen to be in your discipleship group are ultimately Christ's followers, not yours. They should imitate you only to the extent that you are imitating Jesus. Don't try to create clones of yourself. Everyone's personality is different. Each person approaches faith and life in ways that you might not.

▶ The spiritual success or failure of those in your group is not—ultimately—your responsibility. Your responsibility is to be faithful. *God is in charge of outcomes.* Don't take credit for "dynamic" disciples; don't shoulder excessive blame for "followers who falter or fail."

What to Expect in a Discipleship Group

Something very powerful happens when Christians who are eager to grow in their faith commit to:

▶ "Do life together" for a season.

▶ Gather regularly to open God's Word and wrestle with what it means to follow Jesus.

▶ Trust the Spirit of God to bring about transformation in and through them.

Here's a list of five things you can expect if you participate in a discipleship group:

1. **You'll be surprised.** When we dig deeply and ponder prayerfully, we discover things about God, about walking with Christ, and about ourselves that we never knew. Disciples should be curious and open.

2. **You'll be transformed.** Jesus promised that those who are spiritually hungry and thirsty would be satisfied (Matthew 5:6). Disciples can expect to know God better and grow in the faith.

3. **You'll be encouraged.** Nothing is more inspiring than being in a group where the members are experiencing transformation and are being used by Jesus to make an eternal difference in the world. Disciples must be committed and faithful to build each other up in the faith.

4. **You'll encounter resistance.** The enemy of our souls doesn't want us growing in the faith. He will pull out all the stops to oppose, distract, and tempt us. Disciples have to be wary and persistent.

5. **You'll be corrected.** The more we study God's Word, the more we realize that many of our notions about life and the spiritual life are simply wrong. Disciples need to be humble and teachable.

If you are up for all that, here are five important challenges:

1. **Be committed.** The old saying is true: You get out what you put in. Show up. When you miss a group meeting, others can't benefit from what God is teaching you. But don't just attend. Merely showing up to meetings doesn't lead to growing up in the faith. Study. Ponder. Wrestle. Then come prepared to participate.

2. **Be authentic.** It's always tempting to try to make ourselves look better—more spiritual, more solid, etc.—than we really are. But no one benefits from that kind of dishonesty. You don't need to share your deepest secrets, but be a truth-teller even when the truth is hard or ugly. Often one member's transparency and vulnerability can set the tone for an entire group. Be that person!

3. **Be trustworthy.** Help make the group a safe place. Adapt the "Vegas philosophy": *What's said in the group stays in the group.* Don't blab the secrets of others. There's no quicker way to kill a group.

4. **Be realistic.** Groups aren't heaven on earth. You won't "click" with everyone. Some nights the discussions will drag—or you'll come away with more questions than you had when you showed up. That's okay. Remember discipleship is a lifelong process, not an eight- or thirty-week program. Hang in there. Long journeys take a lot of little steps.

5. **Be prayerful.** Jesus said, "Apart from me, you can do nothing" (John 15:5). Without the presence of Christ, your group will be a mere meeting. But if, in a spirit of faith and surrender, you summon and submit to the infinite power of God, who knows what might happen?